SUPPLEMENT TO

SOUTH CAROLINA MARRIAGES

1688-1820

SUPPLEMENT TO

SOUTH CAROLINA MARRIAGES

1688-1820

Compiled by
BRENT H. HOLCOMB

GENEALOGICAL PUBLISHING Co., Inc.

NOTE

HIS IS A SUPPLEMENT to *South Carolina Marriages 1688-1799* and *South Carolina Marriages 1800-1820,* published in 1980 and 1981 respectively. It is based on a variety of sources from around the state, some of which were overlooked in preparing the previous volumes and others which have come to light since the publication of those volumes. In all, over 1,000 new entries are included, with brides and other persons mentioned in the records listed separately in the index.

BRENT H. HOLCOMB, C.A.L.S.
Columbia, South Carolina

SOURCES

Cedar Springs ARP Records
Records of Cedar Springs Associate Reformed Presbyterian Church (Abbeville County). Published in *The South Carolina Magazine of Ancestral Research (SCMAR)*.

CH CH PR
Christ Church Parish Register. Published in *The South Carolina Historical and Genealogical Magazine (SCH&G)*.

Darl MB
Darlington District Marriage Bonds. Originals in the Darlington County Courthouse. Published in *The South Carolina Magazine of Ancestral Research (SCMAR)*.

Fairfield Deed Book
Fairfield County Deed Books (followed by volume and page number). In S.C. Archives.

George Cooper Session Book
Records of the Session of Salem (Black River) Presbyterian Church (Sumter District). Published as a separate volume.

Hayne Records
Records kept by Col. Isaac Hayne (Charleston). Published in *The South Carolina Historical and Genealogical Magazine (SCH&G)*.

Hezekiah Smith Diary
Diary of a Baptist minister ordained in South Carolina in 1763. Revisited South Carolina in 1769.

Horry MB
Marriage bonds and licenses from Horry District. Published in *The South Carolina Magazine of Ancestral Research (SCMAR)*.

Mar Set
Marriage Settlements (followed by volume and page number). A series in the S.C. Archives.

Misc Rec
Miscellaneous Records (followed by volume and page number). A series in the S.C. Archives.

Moses Waddell
Journal of Moses Waddell, a minister who served in Anderson, Abbeville, and other counties, and in Georgia.

Newberry Deed Book	Newberry County Deed Books (followed by volume and page number). In Newberry Courthouse.
Spartanburg Deed Book	Spartanburg County Deed Books (followed by volume and page number). On film in the S.C. Archives.
Sptg Journal of the Ordinary	Spartanburg District Journal of the Ordinary (followed by page numbers). Journal of the probate court.
St. Phil Records	Journals, loose papers, etc., in St. Philip's (Episcopal) Church (Charleston). These records are not in the parish registers.

Abercrombie, John of Charles Town, & Sarah Mitchell, widow, of
   same, ___ 1777. Hayne records

Adler, Stolberg of Charles Town, & Ann Rodgaman, ___ 1778.
   Hayne records

Air, James Dr. of Charles Town, & Elis: Legare, of same,
   ___ 1777. Hayne records

Air, William of Charles Town, & Mary Stephenson, of same, 2 Aug
   1770. Hayne records

Aldrich, Robert, merchant, & Ann Haw___ Lebby, 6 June 1811.
   St. Phil records

Alexander, Alexr. of Charles Town, & Rachel Anderson, 30 Oct
   1767. Hayne records

Allen, Revd. Moses of Christ Church Parish, & Elis: Odinsell,
   of Georgia, ___ July 1775. Hayne records

Allison, Hugh Revd. of Charles Town, & Dorothy Smiser, of same,
   11 Jan 1770. Hayne records

Allston, Benjamin Sen. of Waccamaw & Miss Mary Coachman, 18 Dec
   1808. St. Phil records

Allston, John of Winyaw, & Mary Faucheraud, of Charles Town,
   __ June 1764. Hayne records

Allston, William Junr. of Prince George Parish, & Rachel Moore,
   ___ 1775. Hayne records

Allyn, Robert of St. Bartholomews Parish, & Sarah Jerdan, 1 Jan
   1766. Hayne records

Amory, Jn. & Elis: Cantle, widow, __ Jan 1769. Hayne records

Ancrom, George of Charles Town, & Cather: Porcher, of same,
   27 Nov 1769. Hayne records

Anderson, David & Agnus Hill, 11 Oct 1798. Cedar Springs ARP
   Records

Anderson, John of St. Bartholomews Parish, & Beatrix Gordon,
   widow of same, 1 Aug 1767 Hayne records

Arms, William & Louisa Fitzsimons, 15 Feb 1810. St. Phil records

Arpayne, William of Charleston, marble mason, & Jane McClintock,
   of Philadelphia, spinster, 22 Dec 1803. St. Phil records

Artman, Peter, coachmaker, & Margaret Christian Hauser, spinster,
   17 Feb 1806. St. Phil records

Ashby, Thos. of St. Stephens Parish, & Ann Peyre, of same,
   __ May 1772. Hayne records

Askew, Leonard & Sarah Ellis, __ Dec 1772. Hayne records

Assali(t), John Maria Joseph of Charleston, Gen., & Magdalen
   Aimee Gosselin, of same, spinster, 9 July 1803. St. Phil
   records

1

Atkinson, Joseph of Charles Town, & Mary Burrows, of same, 13 Oct 1774. Hayne records

August, John & Mary Cook, of Camden, 10 Aug 1773. Hayne records

Bacot, Peter of Charles Town, & Elis: Hamond, 11 Nov 1764. Hayne records

Bacot, Peter & Mary Eugenia Cochran, 6 Feb 1810. St. Phil records

Badger, Joseph & Mary Forest, __ April 1778. Hayne records

Baillie, George & Joanna Crook, 30 Dec 1766. Hayne records

Baker, Francis of Charles Town, & Ann Simkins, of same, __ Sept 1768. Hayne records

Baker, John of Charles Town, & Amy Legare, of same, 13 Oct 1767. Hayne records

Baker, Richd. Bohun of St. Andrews Parish, & Elis: Miles, widow of St. Bartholomews Parish, ___ 1774. Hayne records

Baker, Stephen of Georgia, & Martha Fuller, of St. Andrews Parish, ___ 1779. Hayne records

Baker, Thomas of Charles Town, & Esther Baker, of St. Andrews Parish, __ April 1766. Hayne records

Baker, William of Charles Town, & Martha Screven of Jas. Island, 17 July 1763. Hayne records

Baker, Wm of St. Bartholomews Parish, & Ann Sanders, widow, of same, 13 Jan 1766. Hayne records

Ball, Isaac & Eliza Catharine Poyas, 22 Nov 1810. St. Phil records

Ballentine, James, merchant of Charles Town, & Sarah Buchannan, 6 March 1772. Hayne records

Barksdale, George of Christ Church Parish, & Mary Daniel, of Charles Town, ___ 1778. Hayne records

Barnwell, John of Beaufort & Eliz. Fenwick, of Charles Town, 30 Jan 1766. Hayne records

Barnwell, Nathaniel of Beaufort & Eliza: Wait of Wadmelaw Island, __ Dec 1768. Hayne records

Baron, Dr. Alexr. of Charles Town, & Sarah Cleiland, of same, 31 Dec 1772. Hayne records

Bayle, Francis & Frances Minott, __ Sept 1771. Hayne records

Baynard, Joseph & Eliz: Hosford, 25 July 1767. Hayne records

Beard, Jno. & Caty McCinny, 13 Sept 1803. Cedar Springs ARP records

Beard, Robert & Mary Colles, of Charles Town, before 30 Nov 1767. Hayne records

Beaufort, John Dedier & Margt Cook, widow, of St. Helenas Parish, 19 July 1778. Hayne records

Bee, Joseph of St. Pauls Parish, & Ester Ferguson, of St. Bartholomews Parish, 2 Oct 1766. Hayne records

Bee, Joseph of James Island & Elis: Sandaford, of same, __ Oct 1770. Hayne records

Bee, Thos. Esqr., planter & attorney, of Charles Town, & Sarah McKensie, widow of same, 16 March 1773. Hayne records

Beekman, Bernard & Elis: Scott, widow, 14 Dec 1769. Hayne records

Belin, Peter of Santee, & Elis: Gwinnet, of Georgia, 26 March 1779. Hayne records

Bell, Thomas & Anne Murray, __ 1767. Hayne records

Bellamy, William of St. Pauls Parish, & Martha Baker, widow of Dorchester, __ 1776. Hayne records

Bellinger, Edmund of St. Bartholomews Parish, & Mary Cossens of Georgia, 15 March 1767. Hayne records

Bennet, John & Mary Godfrey, __ 1777. Hayne records

Bentham, James, of Charles Town, & Eleanor Philips, widow, of Jamaica, 5 May 1773. Hayne records

Bentham, James of Charles Town, & Mary Hardy, __ 1775. Hayne records

Berwick, John of Charles Town, & Ann Ash, widow of St. Pauls Parish, 2 Jan 1774. Hayne records

Blair, John & Polly McCullock, 28 Dec 1803. Cedar Springs ARP records

Blake, Jno of Charles Town, & Margt. Mercier, of same, 23 Nov 1777. Hayne records

Blakie, George & Eliz: Rosse, widow, of Charles Town, 22 Nov 1767. Hayne records

Blamyer, Wm. & Elis: Lesesne of St. Thomas Parish, __ 1779. Hayne records

Blott, Jno. of Charles Town, & Ann Parks, widow, __ Jan 1770. Hayne records

Blymer, William Jr. & Miss Frances Pogson, 2 Nov 1809. St. Phil records

Bole, Thomas of St. Georges Parish, & Jane Clifford, of St. Bartholomews Parish, 22 July 1766. Hayne records

Bonneau, Francis & Hannah Elfe, of Charles Town, __ 1779. Hayne records

Bonneau, Josiah of Charles Town, & Susan. Eberson of St. Bartholomews Parish, 20 Sept 1774. Hayne records

Boomer, John of Charles Town, & Elisabeth Cleator, widow, of same, 11 Aug 1774. Hayne records

Boone, Capers & Mary Boyd, of Charles Town, ___ 1779. Hayne records

Boower, Jeremiah of Charles Town, & Christina Miller, 6 Sept 1774. Hayne records

Boquet, Peter of Charles Town, & ___ McLaughlan, of St. Pauls Parish, __ June 1769. Hayne records

Boswood, James, blacksmith of Edmundsbury & Mary Jackson, of Jacksonburg, 20 Sept 1770. Hayne records

Boswood, Samuel of St. Bartholomews Parish & Sarah Hippe, of same, 29 April 1766. Hayne records

Bottiton, Peter & Mary Air, widow, of Charles Town, ___ 1777. Hayne records

Bounetheau, Peter of Charles Town, & Elis: Weyman, of same, ___ 1777. Hayne records

Bourdeaux, Daniel of Charles Town, & Martha Smith, of same, 11 Jan 1770. Hayne records

Bourdeaux, Mons(?), & Amy Williams, 24 Nov 1808. St. Phil records

Bowen, Rev. Nathaniel, & Margaret Blake, spinster, 5 Feb 1805. St. Phil records

Bower, Edward of St. Pauls Parish, & Mary Hyatt of St. Bartholomews Parish, 29 April 1766. Hayne records

Bower, Wm., watchmaker of Charles Town, & Catherine Lind, widow, of same, __ Oct 1772. Hayne records

Boyce, Alexr. Capt. 6th Regt. & Cath Othelia McAllister, widow, 28 Dec 1778. Hayne records

Bradwell, John & Elis: Lloyd, 30 March 1775. Hayne records

Brailsford, Jno. of Charles Town, & Eliza: Muncreef, of same, 30 Nov 1769. Hayne records

Brailsford, Joseph of Prince Williams Parish, & Eliza: McPherson, of same, 3 May 1770. Hayne records

Brewton, John, merchant of Charles Town, & Mary Weyman, of same, 8 Jan 1771. Hayne records

Brightman, George & Harriet Blewer, 20 June 1808. St. Phil records

Brisbane, James, planter of Charles Town, & Sarah Stanyarne, of Johns Island, 24 May 1772. Hayne records

Brisbane, Wm. of Charles Town, & Eunace Stevens, of St. Andrews Parish, __ April 1768. Hayne records

Brockington, John & Mary Fowler, __ May 1773. Hayne records

Broughton, Andrew of Charles Town, & Sarah Glaze, of same, ___ Jan 1771. Hayne records

Broughton, Thos of St. Johns Parish, & Elis: Lesesne of Danl. Island, ___ 1774. Hayne records

Broughton, Thomas of St. Johns Parish, & Susannah Donnom, of Charles Town, 18 Nov 1779. Hayne records

Brown, John, of Johns Island, & Elis. Graves, of James Island, 7 Feb 1771. Hayne records

Browne, Francis & Mary Boone, 21 May 1766. Hayne records

Brownson, Nathanl. Dr. of Georgia, & Elis: Martin, widow, of St. Bartholomews Parish, ___ 1774. Hayne records

Bruce, David, merchant of Charles Town, & Eleanor Dryden, 7 April 1765. Hayne records

Bruce, Donald of Orangeburgh, & Margaret Lockhart, of same, ___ Feb 1774. Hayne records

Bruyard, Joseph & Jane Rebecca Prioleau, colored, 21 April 1809. St. Phil records

Bryan, James & Mary Sanks, 16 June 1772. Hayne records

Bryan, John of Charles Town, & Rachel Simmons, of same, 24 April 1777. Hayne records

Budd, John, mariner, & Catharine Miller, widow, 8 June 1805. St. Phil records

Buer, Thos of Jacksonburg, & Rachel Baily, widow, of St. Bartholomews Parish, 13 Feb 1766. Hayne records

Bull, Jno. Esqr. of Charles Town, & Eleanor Purry, of Beaufort, 31 March 1768. Hayne records

Bull, Jno. of Charles Town, & Sarah Philips, of Jamaica, 16 July 1769. Hayne records

Bull, Stephen Esqr., planter of Sheldon, & Ann Middleton, widow, of Beaufort, 24 May 1772. Hayne records

Bull, Thomas, carpenter, of Charles Town, & Sarah Simons, of same, 12 May 1771. Hayne records

Bull, Wm. of Charles Town, & Elis: Reid, of St. Bartholomews Parish, 26 Aug 1779. Hayne records

Burger, David of Charles Town, & Cath: Cleator, ___ 1775. Hayne records

Burgher, David of Charles Town, & Mary Nelmes, ___ 1777. Hayne records

Burgoyne, William, druggist, & Eliza Moser, spinster, 6 Dec 1806. St. Phil records

Burks, Frederick of St. Bartholomews Parish, & Ann Taun(?), of same, 13 March 1774. Hayne records

SUPPLEMENT TO SOUTH CAROLINA MARRIAGES 1688-1820

Burn, John Esq. of Charles Town, & Ann Baron, widow, 30 Oct 1767. Hayne records

Burnside, Wm. & Mary Carter, __ Oct 1772. Hayne records

Burt, Wm. of Charles Town, & Ann Jones, ___ 1775. Hayne records

Burton, Isaac Capt. & Ann Remington, of Charles Town, ___ 1775. Hayne records

Bush, John of Charles Town, & Mary Miles, widow, of St. Andrews Parish, ___ 1775. Hayne records

Butler, Joseph & Maria Tash, 25 Oct 1799, by Revd. Thos. Frost. St. Phil records

Butler, Pierce Major of 29th Regit. & Mary Middleton, of Beaufort, 10 Jan 1771. Hayne records

Butler, Williamson, overseer of St. Bartholomews Parish, & Ann Monro, of same, 24 Dec 1773. Hayne records

Byers, Henry & Cath: Delka, ___ 1777. Hayne records

Cabos, Jean & ____, in French, 11 Sept 1792. Mar Set 5: 5-16

Campbell, Hugh of Jacksonburg, & Eliza Reily, of St. Pauls Parish, 16 April 1766. Hayne records

Campbell, McCartan of Charles Town, & Sarah Fenwicke, of same, ___ 1777. Hayne records

Campbell, Richard & ___, 13 Feb 1808. St. Phil records

Campbell, Lord Wm. of Scotland, & Sarah Izard, of Charles Town, 17 April 1763. Hayne records

Cambridge, Tobias of Charles Town, & Elizabeth Wood, of same, ___ 1778. Hayne records

Cape, Brian of Charles Town, & Mary Hetherington, widow, of St. Thomas Parish, 13 May 1770. Hayne records

Capers, Gabriel of St. Thomas Parish, & Mart: Wetherston of Charles Town, 1 Dec 1767. Hayne records

Capers, Gabriel of Christ Church Parish, & Sarah Lloyd, of Charles Town, ___ 1777. Hayne records

Carson, James Esqr. of Johns Island, & Ann Stuart of Beaufort, ___ May 1770. Hayne records

Carson, Wm. of Charles Town, & Rebecca Lloyd, of same, 9 Jan 1770. Hayne records

Carrol, Patrick of St. Bartholomews Parish, & Mary Brown, 6 July 1767. Hayne records

Carver, Jno Lord & Margt Brown, of Goose Creek, 19 Feb 1767. Hayne records

Cassels, James Esqr. of Charles Town, & Ann Mann, of Black River, __ March 1769. Hayne records

6

Cater, Jno. Dr. & Susannah Tubear, __ June 1779. Hayne records

Cattel, Benjn., planter of St. Andrew Parish, & Mary McCall, of Philadelphia, __ July 1772. Hayne records

Cattell, William of St. Andrews Parish, & Sabina Lynch, of Charles Town, 8 March 1767. Hayne records

Cattell, William of Charleston, gentleman, & Mary Ladson, of same, 8 Nov 1803. St. Phil records

Caveneau, James of St. Bartholomews Parish, & Mary Douglas, widow, of same, 3 June 1766. Hayne records

Chalmers, Lionel of Charles Town & Elizabeth Warden, of same, 2 Aug 1766. Hayne records

Champernoun, William, planter of St. Paul's Parish, & Charlotte Mazyck of Charles Town, 4 July 1765. Hayne records

Champneys, John & Ann Livingston, 3 Nov 1763. Hayne records

Chanler, Isaac, M. D. of Charles Town, & Sarah White, __ April 1771. Hayne records

Chestnut, Jno. & Sarah Cantey, of St. Johns Parish, __ June 1770. Hayne records

Chevalier, C. F., dancing master of St. Bartholomew's Parish, & Sarah Fullerton, widow, of same, 1 Sept 1765. Hayne records

Chifelle, Philotheos of Charles Town, & Rebecca Hutchenson, of St. Bartholomews Parish, 17 Sept 1775. Hayne records

Chisolm, Alexr. of Charles Town, & Christiana Chisolm, of same, 5 Oct 1766. Hayne records

Chitteh, Richard, clerk, of Jacksonburg, & Elis: Saunders, of St. Bartholomews Parish, 23 Sept 1773. Hayne records

Choinard, Charles of Charleston, storekeeper, & Catharine Elmour, of same, widow, 22 Sept 1803. St. Phil records

Chovin, Alexr., factor of Charles Town, & Mary Tart of St. Thos Parish, __ Nov 1772. Hayne records

Christie, James & Hepsibah Rose, of St. Pauls Parish, 19 Nov 1768. Hayne records

Clarke, Cap. Arthur, of the Diligence Packet, & Cath: Inglis, of Charles Town, 3 Feb 1774. Hayne records

Clarkson, Dr. Wm. & Ann Hutchinson, ___ 1775. Hayne records

Clayton, Francis & Mary Colcock, 16 Nov 1766. Hayne records

Cleland, William & Ann Barnett, 26 Oct 1809. St. Phil records

Clifford, Charles of St. Bartholomews Parish, & Elis: Perry of St. Pauls Parish, 11 Sept 1777. Hayne records

Clifford, Henry & Frances Ann Slater, 18 Jan 1809. St. Phil records

Clitherall, Dr. James of Charles Town, & Elisabeth Smith, widow, of same, ___ 1775. Hayne records

Coachman, Benjn. of St. George Parish, & Rebecca Singellton, of St. Bartholomews Parish, ___ 1774. Hayne records

Coachman, James, of Peedee, & Ann Johnson, widow, of Charles Town, 6 May 1773. Hayne records

Coates, Thomas & Martha Goodin Stewart, 27 Nov 1810. St. Phil records

Cochran, Thomas & Susannah Hawie, widow, of Charles Town, ___ 1777. Hayne records

Coey, John C. & Jane McBride, 11 Jan 1810. Cedar Springs ARP records

Cogdell, Charles & Jane Wilkie, widow, ___ 1774. Hayne records

Cogdell, George, Captn. 5th Regt., & Mary Stevens, of Charles Town, ___ 1777. Hayne records

Cogdell, Richard Walpole, & Cecile Langlois, spinster, 16 May 1806. St. Phil records

Cohen, Gershom & Rebecca Sarsedas, ___ 1779. Hayne records

Colcock, Jno. of Charles Town, & Amelia Jones, __ Nov 1768. Hayne records

Cole, Richard of Charles Town, & Ann Boomer, of same, ___ 1777. Hayne records

Colt, Wm Saxby, carpenter of St. Bartholomew's Parish, & Elizabeth Millar, of same, 29 Aug 1765. Hayne records

Colzy, L. C. & Angelique Guerin of Charleston, 4 May 1799. Mar Set 4: 96-97

Combee, Thomas, overseer, & Charlotte Collins, free persons of color, 27 June 1805. St. Phil records

Con, James & Jane Gibson, 14 March 1799. Cedar Springs ARP records

Connely, Jeremiah & Mary Haley Connely, 2 May 1810. St. Phil records

Connor, John & Cather: Rolles, of St. Bartholomews Parish, 21 April 1767. Hayne records

Conyers, Clement Capt. 5th Regt., & Frᵃncis Snell, __ March 1778. Hayne records

Cook, James Prov: Surveyor & Sarah Millhouse, of Camden, 15 Sept 1768. Hayne records

Cook, Wilson of St. Bartholomews Parish, & Sarah Newton, widow, of same, 15 Dec 1767. Hayne records

Cooke, George, of Charles Town, & Eleanor Wade, widow, of same, 17 July 1777. Hayne records

Cooper, Joseph of Horry District, & Rachel Mesho, 1 March 1820; William Alford, James Cooper, wit. Horry Co. Marriage Agreement. (Original document at S. C. Archives.)

Cooper, Peter & Mary Stevens, widow, 10 March 1774. Hayne records

Corbett, Thomas of Charles Town, & Margaret Harleston, 8 June 1769. Hayne records

Cordes, John of St. Johns Parish, & Judith Banbury of Charles Town, ___ 1775. Hayne records

Corslett, Chas. Matthews, Ast. Judge, & Ann Grimke, of Charles Town, 17 Dec 1772. Hayne records

Cossens, Edmond & Amelia Rachel Jones, of St. Bartholomews Parish, ___ 1774. Hayne records

Coustiell, Peter of Jacksonburg, & Mary Hext, widow, of St. Bartholomews Parish, ___ 1769. Hayne records

Couturier, Elias, of St. John's Santee (sic), & Henrietta Couturier, of same, 30 April 1807. St. Phil records

Couturier, Isaac, of St. Johns Santee (sic), & Miss Charlotte Hodgson, of Charleston, 2 May 1807. St. Phil records

Couturier, Joseph, planter of St. John's, & Emily Louisa Kirk, spinster, 19 March 1807. St. Phil records

Cowper, Basil of Georgia, & Mary Smith, of Georgia, ___ Feb 1769. Hayne records

Cox, Thomas, of Charleston, coachmaker, & Rachel Chandler, of same, spinster, 5 July 1803. St. Phil records

Crafts, William Senr. & Harrt. B. Poa__y, 19 Sept 1810. St. Phil records

Craig, Sam & Jane Cochran, 30 July 1799. Cedar Springs ARP Records

Crail, Thomas of Charleston, house carpenter, & Susanna Joy, of same, widow, 17 Dec 1803. St. Phil records

Crawford, Enos & Rebecca Dale, 5 Feb 1799. Cedar Springs ARP Records

Creighton, James of Charles Town, & Leslie Anderson of St. Bartholomews Parish, 6 March 1766. Hayne records

Creighton, John of Qt. House, & Mary Murray, 13 April 1774. Hayne records

Creighton, Samuel & Lizey Williamson, blacks, 28 July 1806. St. Phil records

Cripps, Rob: & Mary Trail(?), ___ Jan 1770. Hayne records

Crips, Jno. Splatt of Charles Town, & Elizabeth Farr, of same, 2 June 1778. Hayne records

Crofts, George, merchant of Charles Town, & Eliza: Leger, 14 Feb 1765. Hayne records

SUPPLEMENT TO SOUTH CAROLINA MARRIAGES 1688-1820

Cromwell, Oliver, taylor, of Charles Town, & Elisa: Warham, of same, 15 July 1773. Hayne records

Crosby, Timothy, Bricklayer, & Margaret Vanderhorst of Berkley Co., widow of William Vanderhorst; John Moore, William Ellis of Charles Town, trustees; John Martin, John Jones, wit., __ Jan 1768. Misc Rec. TT, 339-343

Cross, John of Charles Town, & ___ Strother, of same, __ Dec 1773. Hayne records

Crouch, Henry, Clerk of Charles Town, & Josepha Watson, of England, 30 May 1771. Hayne records

Cruger, David Fredk. & Isabella Liston, __ Feb 1778. Hayne records

Cummings, Andrew & Mary Baker, ___ 1775. Hayne records

Cummins, Wm & Ann Watkins, 10 Feb 1766. Hayne records

Cunningham, Andrew of Charles Town, & Margt. Cochran, widow, of St. Bartholomews Parish, 4 Jan 1767. Hayne records

Cunningham, Jas. -- see Evans, Jas.

Cusack, James, of the Customhouse, Beaufort, & Ann Brown, of Goosecreek, 29 April 1773. Hayne records

Dalcho, Charles Frederick, M. D., & Mary Eliza Threadcraft, spinster, 25 Dec 1805. St. Phil records

Dalton, Charles, planter of St. Bartholomews Parish, & Mary Packer (Parker?), 13 June 1773. Hayne records

Darby, James & Margt. Elliott, of St. Philips Parish, 4 May 1773. Hayne records

Dargan, Timothy, of St. Bartholomew's Parish, & Ann Beasley, of same, 19 Feb 1765. Hayne records

Darrel, Capt. Benj. & Kesiah Boone, widow, __ Jan 1772. Hayne records

Darrell, Capt. Edwd. of Bermuda, & Ann Smith, of Charles Town, 15 May 1770. Hayne records

Dart, John, Esqr., attorney of Charles Town, & Henrietta Somers, of same, 20 Dec 1772. Hayne records

Dart, John S., merchant, of Charles Town & Martha Moote, 23 Jan 1765. Hayne records

Davies, Edward, of Savannah, & Rebecca Lloyd, of same, __ March 1779. Hayne records

Davis, Wm. Ransom Capt. 5 Regt. & Eleanora Norville, of Wateree, __ April 1779. Hayne records

Dawney, John & Sarah Storey, 23 Sept 1766. Hayne records

Day, William of St. Bartholomews Parish, & Elisabeth Postell, of same, 3 Sept 1778. Hayne records

Deas, Joseph & Venus Caunou, blacks, 13 June 1806. St. Phil records

Deas, Thomas Hutchinson, merchant, & Caroline Hall, youngest daughter of the late George Abott Hall, 23 Oct 1805. St. Phil records

Debrahm, Wm. Gerard, Surveyor General, & Mary Fenwick, widow, of Charles Town, 18 Feb 1776. Hayne records

Delahowe, Dr. John of Charles Town, & ___ Boyd, widow, of same, 23 April 1767. Hayne records

Delancy, Peter Esqr. of Charles Town, & Elizab: Beresford, of same, 2 Oct 1770. Hayne records

De Lozur, Asa & Ann Hill, 13 April 1809. St. Phil records

Denny, Thomas of Charleston, physician, & Mary Deborah Lee Gowdey, of same, spinster, 13 Nov 1803. St. Phil records

Dent, John Hubert, captn., & Anne Horry, of Jonah(?) Horry, 7 Feb 1809. St. Phil records

DeSaussure, Henry of Prince Williams Parish, & Jane McPhersons of same, 22 Feb 1767. Hayne records

de Treville, Capt. Jno la Boularderie, Artillery, & Sarah Wilkinson, of Port Royal, ___ Dec 1778. Hayne records

Deveaux, Jacob of Charles Town, & Eliza: Barnwell of Beaufort, ___ June 1768. Hayne records

Deveaux, James & Martha Graden, colored persons, 21 Jan 1808. St. Phil records

Dewees, Andrew & Cath: Chicken, ___ 1778. Hayne records

Dewees, Wm. & Frances Forcey, ___ 1778. Hayne records

Dillon, Robt. of Charles Town, & Christian Chiffelle of Purrysburg, 6 Oct 1768. Hayne records

Dobbins, Joseph & Mary Grange, of St. Bartholomews Parish, 8 Jan 1767. Hayne records

Doble, Saml & Sarah Bosomworth, ___ 1779. Hayne records

Dobson, Joseph & Eliza: Nichols, 3 May 1767. Hayne records

Donnom, Jacob of St. Bartholomews Parish, & Catherine Kirk, 10 June 1766. Hayne records

Donnom, James of St. Bartholomews Parish, & Jane Pepper, widow, of St. Lukes Parish, ___ 1774. Hayne records

Dott, David of Charles Town, & Sarah Baker, of Ashley River, 13 Feb 1768. Hayne records

Dougherty, John, plasterer, & Margaret Brown, spinster, 1 Jan 1805. St. Phil records

Doughty, Thomas of Charles Town & Mary Legare, of same, 10 Oct 1768. Hayne records

Doughty, Wm. of Charles Town, & Rachel Porcher, of same, __ Feb 1770. Hayne records

Douglas, David & __ Weatherford, widow, of Augusta, __ 1777. Hayne records

Drayton, Chas. Dr. of Charles Town, & Esther Middleton, of Charles Town, 24 Feb 1774. Hayne records

Drayton, John of Ashley River, & Rebecca Perry, of St. Pauls Parish, __ 1775. Hayne records

Drayton, Stephen Esqr. of St. Lukes Parish, & Elizab: Waring, of Charles Town, __ Jan 1769. Hayne records

Drayton, William of Charleston, attorney, & Miss Anna Gadsden, spinster, 8 Dec 1803. St. Phil records

Drayton, Wm Henry & Dorothy Golightly, both of Charles Town, 29 March 1764. Hayne records

Drose, Isaac of Dorchester & Mary Eli: Drose, of same, __ Dec 1768. Hayne records

Dubois, David & Susannah Moncrieff, of Charles Town, __ July 1777. Hayne records

Dubois, Isaac & Cath: Dutarque of Charles Town, __ March 1777. Hayne records

Dupont, Charles of St. Lukes Parish, & Sarah Coachman, of St. Johns Parish, __ 1777. Hayne records

Dupont, Gideon Junr. & Ann Jackson, both of St. Bartholomew's Parish, 6 Jan 1765. Hayne records

Dupont, Josiah of St. Bartholomews Parish, & Ann Dupont of same, 1 April 1766. Hayne records

Dupre, Francis of Quebec, mariner, & Susanna Peters, of Charleston, widow, 13 Nov 1803. St. Phil records

Dutarque, John of Charles Town, & Lidia Gaillard, of St. Stevens Parish, 24 Aug 1774. Hayne records

Dysart, Cornelius Dr. & Charity Jack, of North Carolina, __ 1778. Hayne records

Easton, William & Susannah Knowlin, of George Town, __ 1774. Hayne records

Eaton, Sam & Providence Jenkins, widow, __ 1775. Hayne records

Eddings, Benjn., planter of Edisto, & Mary Baily, 20 Sept 1765. Hayne records

Edwards, James of Charles Town, & Rebecca Fripp, of St. Helenas Parish, __ 1778. Hayne records

Edwards, John, merchant of Beaufort, & Mary Barksdale, of Spring Island, __ Nov 1773. Hayne records

Edwards, Jno. esqr., merchant of Charles Town, & Rebecca Holmes, widow, of same, 30 Dec 1773. Hayne records

Elder, Dr. Thos. of St. Thomas Parish, & Char. Hartley, of
    same. 1 May 1773. Hayne records

Elfe, Thomas of Charles Town, & Mary Padgett, 29 Oct 1778.
    Hayne records

Elliott, Barnard of Charles Town, & Mary Elliott of St. Pauls
    Parish, 27 April 1766. Hayne records

Elliott, Barnard of Charles Town, & Susannah Smith, of same,
    __ Jan 1776. Hayne records

Elliott, William of Beaufort, & Mary Cuthbert, widow of Georgia,
    __ Jan 1775. Hayne records

Ellis, Nathan & Mary Drysdel, both of Charles Town, 18 Nov 1769.
    Hezekiah Smith diary

Ellis, Thomas of Charles Town, & Ann Glaze, of same, ___ 1775.
    Hayne records

Elstob, Edward of Charleston, baker, & Mrs. Elizabeth Bocquet
    of Charleston, widow, 19 July 1803. St. Phil records

English, And'w & Martha Porter, 18 Oct 1798. Cedar Springs ARP
    Records

Estes, William of Charleston, planter, & Mary Maguire, of same,
    spinster, 23 April 1803. St. Phil records

Estis, Richd. & Mary Hickey, of St. Bartholomews Parish, 22 May
    1773. Hayne records

Eustace, John of St. Bartholomews Parish, & Ann Thomas, widow,
    of same, 12 Jan 1766. Hayne records

Evans, Jas (alias Cunningham), & Martha Givens, of Beaufort,
    4 Feb 1765. Hayne records

Evans, Jno. Capt. & Mary Anderson, ___ 1778. Hayne records

Evans, John Junr. & Sarah Fripp, 26 Nov 1766. Hayne records

Eveleigh, Nicholas of Charles Town, & Mary Shubrick, of same,
    5 May 1774. Hayne records

Eveleigh, Thos., merchant of Charles Town, & Ann Simmons, of
    same, 23 March 1773. Hayne records

Fardo, George Jno. of Charles Town, & Elis: Godfrey, of St.
    Bartholomews Parish, ___ 1775. Hayne records

Farr, Nathaniel of St. Pauls Parish, & Elis: Smith, widow, of
    same, ___ 1779. Hayne records

Farr, Thomas of Charles Town, & Eliz: Waring, of same, 18 Nov
    1773. Hayne records

Fayoll, John of Charleston, merchant, & Amelia Clement of same,
    spinster, 13 Nov 1803. St. Phil records

Fayssoux, James & Elizabeth Cripps, spinster, 16 Dec 1807.
    St. Phil records

Fayssoux, Peter, M. D. of Charles Town, & Sarah Wilson, of same, 29 Jan 1772. Hayne records

Fayssoux, Peter Dr. of Charles Town, & Ann Johnson, widow, of St. Pauls Parish, ___ 1777. Hayne records

Ferguson, Thos. of St. Pauls Parish, & Elis: Rutledge, widow, of Charles Town, 4 Aug 1774. Hayne records

Ferguson, Thos of St. Pauls Parish, & Ann Wragg, ___ 1777. Hayne records

Findlay, Wm of St. Bartholomews Parish, & Mary Boswood, of same, 28 Jan 1766. Hayne records

Fitch, James, of St. Pauls Parish, & Helen Campbell, of Charles Town, 28 July 1764. Hayne records

Fitts, Michael of St. Luke's Parish, Beaufort Dist., & Mary Margaret Taylor, of same, widow.... 19 Oct 1797. Mar Set 5: 392-4

Fitzgerald, Dr. Alexr. of North Carolina & ___ Beatty, widow, of St. Bartholomews Parish, 11 May 1769. Hayne records

Fitzpatrick, Edmond & Sarah Potter, widow, of Charles Town, ___ 1777. Hayne records

Flagg, George of Charles Town, & Mary Anderson, of same, __ July 1770. Hayne records

Flagg, William, mariner, & Jane Imer, spinster, 21 Dec 1806. St. Phil records

Foley, Thos, Capt. of Ship Escorte, & Catherine Melechamps, of St. Andrews Parish, 4 Nov 1764. Hayne records

Folk, John & Eve Margaret Dickert, 23 Oct 1798, by Rev. Andrew Loretz, minister of the Dutch Presbiterian Church in Newberry Co. Wit: Peter Dickert, Michael Dickert Senr. Newberry Deed Book D, p. 134

Folker, John Hinds & Eliza Lloyd, of Joseph Lloyd, King St., 12 May 1811. St. Phil records

Forbis, Jas. & Mary Thompson, 25 Oct 1798. Cedar Springs ARP Records

Ford, Adam & Sarah Bacot, blacks, 13 June 1806. St. Phil records

Ford, John Senr & Catharine Grace, widow, of Tyger River, Spartanburg Co, 16 April 1792. Wit: John Bruton, Catharine Bruton, Richard Cox, George Grace. Spartanburg Deed Book C, 43-4

Forshaw, Edward, taylor, of Jacksonburg, & Elizabeth Price, widow, of St. Bartholomews Parish, 20 March 1771. Hayne records

Fraser, James, of Prince Williams Parish, & Margt. Prioleau, of same, 2_ Feb 1767. Hayne records

Fraser, John of Charles Town, & Mary Stobo, of Willtown, 23 June 1771. Hayne records

Freer, Solomon of Johns Island & Ann Mathewes, widow, of
  Charles Town, 1 Feb 1777. Hayne records

Friday, William & Lucy Cannon, blacks, 28 July 1806. St. Phil
  records

Frierson, John & Walne Davis, ___ 1775. Hayne records

Fripp, William Chaplin, planter of St. Helena's & Eliza Hann
  Edwards, dau. of James Edwards, 15 May 1806. St. Phil
  records

Fuller, Nathaniel of St. Andrews Parish, & Ann Fuller, of same,
  ___ April 1768. Hayne records

Fuller, Thos. of St. Andrews Parish, & Elis: Miles, widow,
  7 Sept 1766. Hayne records

Fulmer, John, coachmaker, & Ann Arms, spinster, 10 March 1805.
  St. Phil records

Gabbeau, Caesar & Lucy Cannon, blacks, 1 July 1806. St. Phil
  records

Gabeau, John & Susannah Hartman, 15 Oct 1807. St. Phil records

Gadsden, Christopher Genl. of Charles Town, & Ann Wragg, of
  same, ___ 1776. Hayne records

Gadsden, Christopher & Mary Sidney Ashe, 21 Feb 1810. St. Phil
  records

Gadsden, Thos. Capt. 1st Regt. & Martha Fenwicke, of Charles
  Town, 15 Oct 1778. Hayne records

Gaillard, David, planter, & Joanna Dubois, ___ Sept 1773.
  Hayne records

Gaillard, Peter, planter, & Rebecca Weyman Foster, spinster,
  25 May 1807. St. Phil records

Gamewell, John & Delilah Booth, 1 Dec 1812; Silvius. Sweet,
  bondsman. Horry MB

Garden, Benjn, planter, of Prince William's Parish, & Amelia
  Goddin, of St. George's Parish, 17 Jan 1765. Hayne records

Garner, William, planter of St. Pauls Parish, & Sarah Murray,
  of St. Bartholomews Parish, ___ Dec 1771. Hayne records

Germane, Edwd & Sara Cahusac, ___ Nov 1771. Hayne records

Gervais, Jno Lewis, merchant of Charles Town, & Mary Sinclair,
  of same, 7 Oct 1773. Hayne records

Geyer, John & Mary Oakford, 20 Jan 1810. St. Phil records

Gibbes, John Walters of Charles Town, & Amar: Badely, of same,
  ___ 1776. Hayne records

Gibbes, Robt Esqr. of John's Island & Sarah Reeves, of Beaufort,
  ___ June 1764. Hayne records

Giles, Othniel of Charles Town, & Lady Jane Colleton, widow, of St. Johns Parish, ___ 1777. Hayne records

Gillespie, David of Charles Town, & Mary Rogers, widow, of same, 14 May 1770. Hayne records

Gilley, Robert of Clarendon County, carpenter, & Susannah Cobia, widow of Michael Cobia, 10 March 1795; James Richbourg Junr., William Richbourg, trustees; John Richbourg, Temperance Nisbett, wit. Mar Set 5: 264-266

Gillon, Alexr. of Charles Town, & Mary Cripps, widow of same, 6 ___ 1766. Hayne records

Gilmor, Robert Junr., Esqr., of Baltimore, & Sarah Reeve Ladson, dau. of Maj. James Ladson, 9 April 1807. St. Phil records

Girardeau, Jno. Bohum of St. Bartholomews Parish, & Hannah Maybank, widow of same, 18 Aug 1768. Hayne records

Glaze, John of Dorchester & Margt. McNeil, widow, of same, ___ 1775. Hayne records

Glaze, William of Charles Town, & Ann Nevin, widow, of same, 23 Aug 1778. Hayne records

Gleize, Henry & Susannah Peyre, 17 Nov 1808. St. Phil records

Glen, John Esqr., attorney of Savannah, & Sarah Jones of same, ___ Nov 1771. Hayne records

Glen, Wm. of Charles Town, & Martha Miller, of St. Thomas Parish, 5 April 1770. Hayne records

Glesson, Jacob & Ann Hipp, 20 Dec 1764. Hayne records

Glover, Henry Charles & Harriott Ann Cart, 15 March 1810. St. Phil records

Glover, Capt. Joseph of St. Bartholomews Parish, & Ann Webb, widow, of same, ___ 1777. Hayne records

Gordon, James of Charles Town, & Cat: Smith, of New York, 10 March 1767. Hayne records

Gough, Richd. & E. Barnwell, ___ 1772. Hayne records

Gould, William & Ann Clark, of St. Bartholomew's Parish, 15 April 1765. Hayne records

Gowrley, John & Elizabeth Rivers, 25 Dec 1769, at Charles Town. Hezekiah Smith diary

Graham, James of Georgia, & Sarah Stuart of Charles Town, 16 July 1767. Hayne records

Grange, Thos, of St. Bartholomew's Parish, & Sarah Singleton of same, 31 Dec 1765. Hayne records

Green, John & Ann King, 28 Dec 1819; Saml. Willson, bondsman; James Coggeshall, Richd. Singleton, wit. Horry MB

Green, Joseph & Hannah Blackwell, 22 Dec 1806; license directed to the Revd. Mr. Jeremiah Norman. Horry MB

Green, Richard Junr. & Frances Davis, 24 March 1804; Silvanus
Sweet, planter, bondsman; license directed to Revd. Mr.
Thos. Humphries; Wm. Hemingway, wit. Horry MB

Greene, Nathanl. of Hiltonhead, & Susanh. Chanler, of Charles
Town, 15 Jan 1770. Hayne records

Greenland, George & Charlotte Warley, __ Dec 1767. Hayne records

Greenland, George of Charles Town, & Martha Simons, of St. James
Santee Parish, __ Dec 1770. Hayne records

Gregory, Wm. & Ann Leacroft, 20 Oct 1765. Hayne records

Greiner, Meinard, merchant, & Mercy Palmer, spinster, 23 May
1805. St. Phil records

Greville, Doctr. Saml. of Charles Town, & Mary Pendarvis, of
St. Pauls Parish, __ Aug 1773. Hayne records

Griffith, Edward of Charles Town, & Martha Miles, of St.
Bartholomews Parish, 19 Nov 1767. Hayne records

Grimball, Thomas, attorney of Charles Town, & Mary Prioleau of
same, 23 June 1765. Hayne records

Grimes, Thomas W. & Charity Nicholson, __ Nov 1798. Moses
Waddel

Gros, John, cabinet mkr., & Elizabeth Cath. Love, spinster,
16 May 1807. St. Phil records

Guerard, Benj. of Charles Town, & Sarah Middleton of Beaufort,
29 Nov 1766. Hayne records

Guerard, David of Santee, & Judith de St. Julien of Charles
Town, 30 Oct 1767. Hayne records

Guerard, David of Santee & Martha Barnwell, of Beaufort, 16
Sept 1770. Hayne records

Guerard, Goddin of Prince Williams Parish, & Ann Mathewes, of
Charles Town, 23 Aug 1769. Hayne records

Guerry, Stephen of St. Thomas Parish, & Frances Michau, ___ 1779.
Hayne records

Guinard, Jno Gabriel, of High Hills, & Elis. Sanders, of same,
___ May 1779. Hayne records

Gunter, Edward Apothecary of Charles Town, & Martha Mellichamp,
of St. Andrews Parish, 29 March 1772. Hayne records

Hacket, Dr. Michael of St. Paul's Parish, & Eliza White, widow,
of Monks Corner, 14 Feb 1765. Hayne records

Hagar, Richard, shopkeeper, & Henrietta Donavan, spinster,
17 March 1805. St. Phil records

Haggot, Wm. of England & ___ Walter, 13 Dec 1767. Hayne records

Hagood, John, merchant & Elizabeth Campbell, widow, 8 Nov 1809.
St. Phil records

Haig, George Dr., of St. Paul's Parish, & Sarah McKewn, of same, 2 May 1769. Hayne records

Hall, Daniel of Charles Town, & Susannah Mathewes of Johns Island, 21 Feb 1775. Hayne records

Hall, Geo. Abbot & Lois Mathewes, 14 Feb 1764. Hayne records

Hall, John of Charles Town, & Mary Ann Dodd, of same, 10 April 1774. Hayne records

Hall, Nathl. of Georgia, & Mary Gibbons, ___ 1774. Hayne records

Hall, Thomas & Dorothy Jones, of St. Bartholomew's Parish, 7 Feb 1765. Hayne records

Hamilton, David & Isabella Weems, 4 May 1802. Cedar Springs ARP Records

Hamilton, Joseph, aged 68, of Edisto & Elis: Dunmire, aged 61 of same, ___ March 1773. Hayne records

Hanahan, Edward & Elis: Doyley, 13 Dec 1778. Hayne records

Hannahan, Wm. of Edisto, & Mary Rippon, of same, ___ 1774. Hayne records

Hardy, Wm., watchmaker, of Charles Town, & ___ Cotton, 21 June 1778. Hayne records

Harleston, John of St. Johns Parish, & Elis: Faucheraud, of Charles Town, 24 April 1766. Hayne records

Harleston, John of St. Johns Parish, & Elis: Lynch of Santee, ___ May 1777. Hayne records

Harmon, John, baker of Jacksonburg, & Martha Peter, widow, of same, 22 July 1773. Hayne records

Harris, Chas. & Elis: Christie, 31 Dec 1773. Hayne records

Harris, Charles of Charles Town, & Ann Padgett, 25 June 1778. Hayne records

Hart, John & Elis: Holson, widow, ___ 1779. Hayne records

Hart, Revd. Oliver of Charles Town, & Ann Grimball, widow, of same, 5 April 1774. Hayne records

Hart, Oliver Dr. of Charles Town, & Sarah Brockington, of Charles Town, 19 Nov 1778. Hayne records

Hartly, George Harland, organist of St. Philips church, & Elis: Cummings, of Charles Town, ___ July 1776. Hayne records

Hartly, Thomas of Stono & Mary Hyatt, widow of St. Bartholomews Parish, 26 March 1767. Hayne records

Harvey, Wm., waggoner of St. Bartholomews Parish, & Mary Wheatly, widow, of Jacksonburg, 19 July 1773. Hayne records

Hasell, Andrew & Hannah Cochran Ashe, 21 Feb 1810. St. Phil records

Hatfield, John, chandler, of Charles Town, & Sarah Swallows, of Charles Town, 6 Jan 1765. Hayne records

Hawie, Robert & Susannah Lesesne, 14 Dec 1769. Hayne records

Hayne, Isaac, planter of St. Bartholomew's Parish, & Eliza: Hutson of Charles Town, 18 July 1765. Hayne records

Hazel, James Junr. & Susan Foissin, of Santee, 6 March 1767. Hayne records

Hazell, Andrew & Mary Milner, 15 Oct 1778. Hayne records

Heatly, Chas. Capt. & Ann Sabb, __ April 1776. Hayne records

Hederick, John & Ann Burns, 1 Jan 1809. St. Phil records

Hemmet, Thomas of Charles Town, & Charlotte Kirk, widow, __ 1776. Hayne records

Henderson, Daniel, of Charleston, whitesmith, & Jesse Kirkwood, of same, widow, 4 Dec 1803. St. Phil records

Henderson, James Revd. of Edisto, & Hannah Sands, widow, of Charles Town, __ 1774. Hayne records

Hendlin, Thomas & Mary Arnold, widow __ 1777. Hayne records

Heriott, George of George Town, & Sarah Tucker, of Charles Town, __ 1775. Hayne records

Hervey, James, of Charles Town, & Mary Gibbes, of St. Bartholomews Parish, 23 March 1769. Hayne records

Hewatt, Andw, wine merchant of Charles Town, & Cath: Elliott, widow of same, 19 June 1773. Hayne records

Hext, Jno., of St. Pauls Parish, & Elis: Cheesborough, of St. Bartholomews Parish, __ 1779. Hayne records

Hext, Philip of St. Bartholomews Parish, & Susan. Webster, widow, of same, __ 1774. Hayne records

Heyward, Daniel, planter of St. Helena & Margt. Heyward, of Charles Town, __ May 1771. Hayne records

Heyward, Daniel Coln., planter of St. Helenas Parish, & Elizabeth Simmons of Charles Town, 8 Sept 1771. Hayne records

Heyward, Thos. Captn. of ye Ship Martin, & Ann Sinclair, of Charles Town, __ March 1770. Hayne records

Heyward, Thos., Esqr., planter & atty. of Charles Town, & Elisa: Mathews, of same, 20 April 1773. Hayne records

Heyward, Willm. of St. Lukes Parish, & Hannah Shubrick, of Charles Town, 1 Jan 1778. Hayne records

Hibben, Andrew of Charles Town, & __ Winwood, (widow) of Christ Church Parish, 8 Jan 1766. Hayne records

Higgins, George, Capt. of the Snow Portland, & Eliz: Collis, of Charles Town, 12 Feb 1769. Hayne records

Hill, Revd. & Susannah Green, widow, of Charles Town, ___ 1776.
Hayne records

Hoare, William of New York, & Miss Sarah Legare, dau. of James
Legare (no date), by Revd. J. Dewar Simons. St. Phil records

Hoey, John, of Charleston, grocer, & Mary Estes, of same,
widow, 1 March 1810 (original marriage license). St. Phil
records

Hogg, Alexr. of Charles Town, & Eunace Brisbane, widow, of same,
18 July 1773. Hayne records

Holman, Samuel & Agnes Mitchel, free persons of color, 25 Sept
1805. St. Phil records

Holmes, Daniel & Elisab: Freer, of Johns Island, ___ 1775.
Hayne records

Holmes, Isaac of Charles Town, & Elizabeth Air, widow, of same,
5 Jan 1779. Hayne records

Holmes, John & Helen Boomer, 5 Nov 1778. Hayne records

Honywood, Arthur of Charleston, engraver, & Susanna Mills, of
same, spinster, 12 June 1803. St. Phil records

Hope, Wm, merchant of Beaufort & Mary Smith, of same, 25 Oct
1765. Hayne records

Hopkins, Samuel of Charles Town, & Frances Dandridge, widow of
same, 21 June 1770. Hayne records

Hopkins, William of Charles Town, & Eliza: Welch, of same,
12 Aug 1770. Hayne records

Horlbeck, John & Elis: Gallman, widow, __ Feb 1769. Hayne
records

Horri, Elias Esqr., of Prince George Parish, & Elizab:
Brandford, of Charles Town, 15 Nov 1770. Hayne records

Horry, Daniel, Esq., of Santee, & Harriet Pinckney of Charles
Town, __ Feb 1768. Hayne records

Horry, Thos, planter of Santee, and Ann Branford of same,
13 June 1772. Hayne records

Hort, Wm., factor of Charles Town, & Alice Gibbes, of Christ
Church Parish, __ Jan 1772. Hayne records

Howard, Major R. & Harriet Lee, 19 April 1810. St. Phil records

Howley, Richd. of Charles Town, & Sarah Fuller, widow, of St.
Andrews Parish, __ 1775. Hayne records

Huger, Benjn. of Charles Town, & Mary Golightly, of St.
Bartholomews Parish, 1 Aug 1767. Hayne records

Huger, Benj., Esqr., planter of Charles Town, & Mary Kinlock,
of same, 1 Dec 1772. Hayne records

Huger, Danl of Charles Town, & Sabina Elliott, of same, 1 Nov
1772. Hayne records

Huger, John of Charles Town, & Charlotte Motte, of same, 15 March 1767. Hayne records

Hughes, Henry of Santee, & Susannah Bothwell, widow, ___ 1779. Hayne records

Hughes, John & Ann Dinsley, 28 Dec 1765. Hayne records

Hull, Wm., planter of Euhany, & Sarah Field, widow, of Chehaw, ___ Aug 1772. Hayne records

Hume, James of Georgia, & Mary Tannard, of same, ___ May 1770. Hayne records

Hume, Robert, of Goose creek, & Susannah Hume of St. Thos Parish, 24 April 1766. Hayne records

Hunt, Joseph, planter of St. Bartholomews Parish, & Mary Gray of same, ___ May 1772. Hayne records

Hunt, Thomas, atty-at-law, & Louisa Gaillard, spinster, 6 Jan 1805. St. Phil records

Hurst, Robert of Goosecreek, & Jane Egan, of Black river, ___ Sept 1772. Hayne records

Hutchinson, Mathias & Jane Perdriau, ___ June 1769. Hayne records

Hutchinson, Mathias of Charles Town, & Elis: Brandford, widow, of St. Georges Parish, ___ 1777. Hayne records

Hutson, Thomas & Esther Maine, 21 Oct 1773. Hayne records

Imrie, Charles & Elis: Russell, widow, ___ Sept 1771. Hayne records

Imrie, John & Margt. Esmand, widow, 2 Oct 1774. Hayne records

Inglis, Alexr., merchant of Georgia, & Mary Deas, of Charles Town, 27 April 1773. Hayne records

I'on, Jacob of Christ Church Parish, & Mary Ashby, of St. Thomas Parish, ___ 1775. Hayne records

I'on, Richard & Elizabeth Bond, 29 April 1745. Ch Ch PR

Ioor, George & Frances Guignard, ___ 1779. Hayne records

Izard, Ralph & Alice Delancy of New York, 1 May 1767. Hayne records

Izard, Walter of St. Georges Parish, & Mary Fenwicke, of Charles Town, ___ Nov 1779. Hayne records

Jamieson, James, merchant of Charles Town, & Rebecca Simons, of same, 25 May 1773. Hayne records

Jaudon, Elias & Mary Dixon, of Prince Williams Parish, ___ Feb 1770. Hayne records

Jaudon, Saml & Elis: Atkinson, ___ 1775. Hayne records

Jeanneret, Thomas & Rhina Toomer, colored persons, 10 June
    1807. St. Phil records

Jenkins, Charles James & Mary Ann Crowson, 12 Aug 1806; Lewis
    Daniell, bondsman; Jacob Crowson, wit; license directed to
    the Revd. Mr. Norman. Horry MB

Jenkins, Rev. Edward of St. Bartholomews Parish, & Susan: Reid,
    widow, of same, 31 July 1773. Hayne records

Jennings, Jno. Capt. of Bermuda & Mary Dutarque of St. Thos'
    Parish, 20 Jan 1765. Hayne records

Jervey, Thomas of Charles Town, & Grace Hall, of same, __ Aug
    1770. Hayne records

Jocelin, Henry of Charleston, cabinet maker, & Mary Bredlove,
    of same, spinster, 25 Dec 1803. St. Phil records

Johnson, Saml. & Mary Ficklin, __ Jan 1773. Hayne records

Johnson, William of Charles Town, & Sarah Nightingale, of same,
    15 May 1769. Hayne records

Johnson, Wm., planter of Longbay, & Ann Smith, of St. Pauls
    Parish, 20 March 1773. Hayne records

Johnston, Andrew, planter, of Prince Georges Parish, & Sarah
    McKewn, of St. Pauls Parish, 25 Feb 1772. Hayne records

Johnston, Charles of Charles Town, & Mary McKenzie, of same,
    17 June 1770. Hayne records

Jones, James, of St. Bartholomews Parish, & Ann Vinson of same,
    15 June 1767. Hayne records

Jones, John & Marg. Hamilton, 14 May 1767. Hayne records

Jones, John of Charles Town, & Mary Sharp, of Jacksonburg, 28
    Dec 1769. Hayne records

Jones, Thos. of Charles Town & Mary Townsend, of same, 4 June
    1766. Hayne records

Jones, Thomas & Eliza Trouss(?), widow, 13 Jan 1810. St. Phil
    records

Jordon, James, overseer of St. Bartholomews Parish, & Sarah
    Christie, of St. Bartholomews Parish, __ Oct 1770. Hayne
    records

Karwon, Thos. Crafton, merchant, aged 25, & Mary Marion, aged
    65, of St. Thomas Parish, 16 Jan 1773. Hayne records

Karwon, Thos. & Cath: Bonneau. ___ 1774. Hayne records

Keenhardt, William & Deborah Halliday, __ Sept 1810. St. Phil
    records

Keith, Alexr. Capt. of 5th Regt. & Susannah Bulline, of Ashley
    River, 2 Dec 1779. Hayne records

Kennedy, Lionel Henry, atty-at-law, & Mary Ann Jane Stephens,
    9 June 1811. St. Phil records

Kennedy, Dr. Mathew of Jacksonburg, & Ann Glass, of St. Pauls Parish, 8 April 1773. Hayne records

Kenward, Jno. of St. Augustine, & Mary Eli: Welchuysen, of Charles Town, 17 Aug 1773. Hayne records

Kershaw, Eli of Rockingham, & Mary Canty, of Camden, 19 Nov 1769. Hayne records

Kidd, Archd. & Elis: Morrison, 16 Nov 1802. Cedar Springs ARP Records

King, James, mariner, & Mary Rose Love, spinster, 24 March 1805. St. Phil records

Kirk, Edward, merchant of New Province, & Charlotte Bennit, of Charles Town, __ Nov 1770. Hayne records

Ladson, James Capt. 1st Regt., & Judith Smith, of Charles Town, 1 Oct 1778. Hayne records

Ladson, Joseph, planter & Martha Hampton, both of St. Bartholomews Parish, 22 Nov 1764. Hayne records

Ladson, Robt. Esq., planter & attorney of Charles Town, & Sarah Fleming, of same, 18 March 1773. Hayne records

Ladson, Thomas of Johns Island & Mary Cole, of same, __ Dec 1768. Hayne records

Ladson, Wm., planter of St. Pauls Parish, & Jane Freer, of Johns Island, __ Dec 1773. Hayne records

Lafar, Joseph of Charles Town, & Cath Boillat, of same, ___ 1778. Hayne records

Lafond, Francis C. N. of Charleston, goldsmith, & Sophia Smith, widow, 7 Dec 1813. (original marriage license) St. Phil records

Lamb, Thomas & Sarah McDonald, 10 Dec 1808. St. Phil records

Lambright, John, shoemaker of St. Bartholomew's Parish, & Sarah Boggs of same, 6 June 1765. Hayne records

La Motte, Anthony of Charles Town, & Dorcas Randall, of same 8 March 1767. Hayne records

Lance, Lambert, merchant of Charles Town, & Ann Magd: Kerne, of same, 21 Feb 1765. Hayne records

Latham, Richard of Charles Town, & Grace Forbes, ___ 1778. Hayne records

Latta, Revd. James of Johns Island, & Sarah Wilson, __ March 1775. Hayne records

Law, John of Connecticut & Mary Glover, widow, of St. Bartholomews Parish, 6 May 1770. Hayne records

Law, Joseph, planter of St. Bartholomew's Parish, & Mary Bradwell, of same, 23 April 1765. Hayne records

SUPPLEMENT TO SOUTH CAROLINA MARRIAGES 1688-1820

Lawrence, Jonathan of Charles Town, & Elis: Daniel, of Daniels
Island, ___ 1777. Hayne records

Lawrence, Stephen of Charles Town, & Jane Givens, of Port Royal,
___ 1779. Hayne records

Lawson, Capt. Jno. of Charleston, mariner & Mary Danford, of
same, spinster, 10 June 1803. St. Phil records

Lebby, Nathaniel of Charleston, block-maker, & Eleanor Mann,
of same, widow, 4 Nov 1803. St. Phil records

Lechmere, Nicholas, Colr. of Beaufort, & Cath. Deveaux, of same,
10 April 1774. Hayne records

Lee, William of Charles Town, & Ann Theus, of same, ___ Feb 1769.
Hayne records

Lee, William, merchant, & Lady Belhaven, 25 May 1807. St.
Phil records

Legare, Benjn. of Charles Town, & Alice Cox, of same, 7 March
1776. Hayne records

Legare, Nathan of Christ Church Parish, & Elis: Daniel, of
Charles Town, ___ 1774. Hayne records

Legare, Samuel of Charles Town, & Eleanor Hoyland, of same,
21 May 1776. Hayne records

Legge, Edward of Ashley Ferry, & ___ Waldren, widow, of St.
Georges Parish, 30 April 1775. Hayne records

Leison(?), James of Charles Town, & Rebecca Hinds, of same,
2 July 1778. Hayne records

Leitch, Andrew of St. Pauls Parish, & Cath: Spooler, widow, of
same, ___ 1778. Hayne records

Lesene, Charles, planter, & Eliza Sergeant, spinster, 20 April
1806. St. Phil records

Lesesne, John & Mary Frederick, 2 July 1778. Hayne records

Leslie, James of Hobcaw, & Mary Stokes, widow, of Charles Town,
22 Sept 1770. Hayne records

Lestargette, Lewis, of Charles Town, & Elis: Burnham Elliott,
of St. Philips Parish, ___ Sept 1773. Hayne records

Lewis, Benja, merchant of West Indies, & Fran: Clau: Timothy, of
Charles Town, ___ Jan 1769. Hayne records

Lightwood, Edwd of Charles Town, & Elizab: Peronneau, of same,
1 Jan 1770. Hayne records

Limmocks, John & Elizabeth Sleigh, both of St. Bartholomews
Parish, 9 Nov 1764. Hayne records

Lind, Thos & Catherine Smith, 30 Dec 1766. Hayne records

Linning, John, planter of Charles Town, & Mary Rivers, of
Wappo, 30 May 1771. Hayne records

Lintot, John & Mary Runnel, ___ 1775. Hayne records

24

Little, Robert, of Jacksonburg, & Ann Hext, widow, of same,
8 June 1769. Hayne records

Logan, Christian Muldred, of Charleston, mercht., & Sarah White
Chandler, of same, spinster, 25 Jan 1803. St. Phil records

Long, Wm. of Charles Town, & Elis: Kirkwood, widow, of same,
___ 1777. Hayne records

Lord, Andrew, merchant of Charles Town, & Ann Gadsden, widow,
of same, 22 Nov 1770. Hayne records

Lord, Archibald Brown, & Mary Guerin Waities, 22 Nov 1810.
St. Phil records

Lovell, Josiah Sturgis, merchant, & Hannah Frances Poinsett,
spinster, 26 May 1806. St. Phil records

Lowndes, Honble Rawlins, planter of Charles Town, & Sarah Jones,
of same, 25 Feb 1773. Hayne records

Loyd, Joseph & Sarah Mitchel, 20 Aug 1766. Hayne records

Lusk, Wm. & Mary McMillian, 1 Sept 1803. Cedar Springs ARP
Records

Lushington, Richard of Charles Town, & Charity Ball, widow, of
same, 9 July 1774. Hayne records

Lynch, Thos Junr., planter of Santee & Elizabeth Shubrick, of
Charles Town, 14 May 1772. Hayne records

McAlpin, John & Susanna Anderson, 5 June 1804; Gilbert McAlpin,
bondsman; license directed to Rev. William Holt; William
Hemingway, wit. Horry MB

McCall, James of Charles Town, & Ann Dart, of same, 27 April
1777. Hayne records

McCall, John of Charles Town, & Charlotte Glen, of same, 9 Nov
1767. Hayne records

McCall, Captn. Jno. of Charles Town, & Ann Lesesne, of Daniels
Island, ___ April 1777. Hayne records

McCants (McKance), and Elizabeth McMeekin, 30 Jan 1802; J.
Davison, wit. Proved in York Dist. Fairfield Deed Book V,
p. 97

McCay, Edward, of St. Stephens Parish, Charleston Dist., & Judith
Piggot, 10 March 1795; Archd McBride, wit. Darl MB

McCorkel, Saml. & Grizel Keir(?), of Jas. Island, ___ July 1772.
Hayne records

McCormick, Richard & Eliza Halliday, ___ Sept 1810. St. Phil
records

McCreery, Joseph & Mary Boggs, 31 March 1803. Cedar Springs
ARP Records

McDaniel, Zachariah & Lucy Shands, 4 April 1817. Sptg Journal
of the Ordinary 1816-1818, p. 25

McFadden, Robert & Leah Lenoir, widow of James Dickey, 6 June
1799. George Cooper Session Book

McFerrin, John & Martha Shanks, 23 Dec 1800. Cedar Springs ARP
Records

McGaw, John & Agness Cochran, 11 Dec 1799. Cedar Springs ARP
Records

McGilvray, William & Ann Hinckley, ___ 1776. Hayne records

McIntosh, Geo. of Georgia, & Ann Houston, of same, ___ May 1772.
Hayne records

McIntosh, Laclan, of St. Andrews Parish, & Elis. Smith, of same,
17 Oct 1765. Hayne records

McKensie, Alexr., patroon & Sarah Whitle, widow, of Jacksonburg,
9 Feb 1773. Hayne records

McKensie, James of Charles Town & Ann Immer, widow of Purrysburg, ___ July 1768. Hayne records

McKensie, John Esqr. of Charles Town, & Sarah Smith, of same,
3 April 1769. Hayne records

McKenzie, Henry & Anna Maria Smith, 6 March 1808. St. Phil
records

McNeil, Dr. Archib: of Charles Town, & Eliza: Postell, of
Dorchester, ___ Sept 1769. Hayne records

McPherson, Isaac of St. Pauls Parish, & Sarah Perry of same,
___ Feb 1776. Hayne records

McPherson, John of Prince Williams Parish, & Susanna Miles, of
St. Pauls Parish, ___ 1776. Hayne records

McPherson, Ulysses, of Prince Williams, & Sarah Laird, of
Charles Town, ___ June 1770. Hayne records

McQueen, Alexr. of Charles Town, & Elis: Fuller, of St. Andrews
Parish, 14 Jan 1774. Hayne records

Mackay, Robert, of Augusta, & ___ Chilcotte, widow of Rhode
Island, ___ Jan 1772. Hayne records

Mackey, Alexr. & Mary Williams, 26 Nov 1766. Hayne records

Macon, John & Charlotte Woodward, 29 Oct 1803; William Woodward,
Ezekiel Sanders, wit. Fairfield Deed Book O, p. 399

Man, John Spencer & Mrs. Ann Barksdale, widow, 11 July 1807.
St. Phil records

March, belonging to Mr. Gordon, & Sarah, belonging to Mrs.
Watson, 21 April 1809. St. Phil records

Marshall, Dr. Francis Walder of James Island, & Mary Hinds, of
Charles Town, ___ Aug 1777. Hayne records

Marshall, John & Miss Maria Metclaff, 8 May 1807. St. Phil
records

Martin, Hawkins of St. Pauls Parish, & _____ Vanderhorst, Christ
Church Parish, 21 Nov 1774. Hayne records

Martin, Richard of St. Bartholomews Parish, & Martha Woodcroft
of same, 6 May 1767. Hayne records

Mathewes, Benjn. of Charles Town, & Sarah Sams, of Johns Island,
__ March 1770. Hayne records

Mathewes, Benjn. Cap. of Johns Island, & Martha Mathewes, of
same, 19 __ 1778. Hayne records

Mathewes, George of Charles Town, & Mary Saltus, of Dorchester,
2 May 1776. Hayne records

Mathewes, Jno. of Goosecreek, & Sally Scott, of Boston, __ Jan
1770. Hayne records

Mathewes, John Esq. of Charles Town, & Mary Wragg of same, 8
Dec 1766. Hayne records

Mathewes, John of Charles Town, & Ann Hervey, of same, 22 Feb
1767. Hayne records

Mathewes, John Raven of Charles Town, & Elis: Holmes of same,
__ June 1775. Hayne records

Mathewes, Wm. of Johns Island & Elis: Coachman, of St. James
Parish, __ Jan 1777. Hayne records

Matthews, William & Mary Bee, 15 Nov 1810. St. Phil records

Maverick, Saml of Charles Town, & Lidia Turpin of same, __ Jan
1772. Hayne records

Mayson, Colo. James of 3 Regt., & Henrietta Hart, of St. Johns
Parish, __ Aug 1776. Hayne records

Mazyck, Alexander of Charles Town, & Charlotte Broughton, of
St. Johns Parish, 15 Nov 1770. Hayne records

Mazyck, Nathaniel Broughton, of Charleston, merchant &
Chritiana Boston Harris, of same, spinster, 27 Jan 1803.
St. Phil records

Mazyck, Paul of Charles Town, & ___ Hamon, of Ireland, ___ 1775.
Hayne records

Mealy, Thos & Jean Foster, 4 Sept 1798. Cedar Springs ARP
Records

Mezzer, David & Sarah Dacosta, ___ 1779. Hayne records

Michie, Alexr. of Charles Town, & Henrietta Carroll, of same,
9 ___ 1766. Hayne records

Middleton, Arthur & Alicia Russell, 9 March 1809. St. Phil
records

Middleton, Henry of Charles Town, & Lady Mary Ainslie, widow,
of St. Georges Parish, ___ 1776. Hayne records

Mitchell, John & Jane Rutledge, 23 March 1809. St. Phil records

Middleton, Thomas, of Crowfield, & Mary Gibbes, of Johns
    Island, __ Nov 1774. Hayne records

Middleton, Thomas, of Crowfield, & Elis: Deas, of Charles Town,
    22 Dec 1778. Hayne records

Miles, Acquilla, of St. Peters Parish, & ___ Dunn, widow of
    Purysburg, __ Sept 1771. Hayne records

Miles, Jno. of St. Bartholomews Parish, & Kesiah Perry, widow,
    of same, 17 Jan 1774. Hayne records

Miles, Robt., planter of Stono, & Elizabeth Smith, of same,
    __ Oct 1772. Hayne records

Miles, Stephen of Cainhoy, & Mary Roche, of St. Thomas Parish,
    22 Sept 1770. Hayne records

Miles, William of Ashepoo, & Mary Elliott, of St. Andrews
    Parish, 26 Oct 1769. Hayne records

Millagan, Jacob of Charles Town, & Margt. Bennet, __ March
    1774. Hayne records

Miller, John David & Jane Righton, ___ 1779. Hayne records

Miller, Saml. & Esther Morgan, ___ 1777. Hayne records

Milligan, Wm., merchant of Charles Town, & Rebecca Stoll, of
    same, 5 Oct 1773. Hayne records

Millis, John & Rebecca Swansey, 31 May 1767. Hayne records

Milner, Solomon of Charles Town, & Ann Ash, of same, ___ 1777.
    Hayne records

Miott, Jno. & Frances Harden, __ Nov 1771. Hayne records

Mitchell, David & Susanna Frierson, __ Dec 1797. George Cooper
    Session Book

Mitchell, John, planter of St. Pauls Parish, & ___ M'Pherson,
    widow, 18 July 1765. Hayne records

Mitchell, Wm., carpenter, & Ruth Thomson, widow, ___ 1779.
    Hayne records

Moncreef, Richard of Charles Town, & Elis: Young, of St. Nath:,
    17 Dec 1778. Hayne records

Moncreef, Robt of Charles Town, & Mary Dewar, of same, 2 April
    1775. Hayne records

Moncrief, Jno. Capt. & Mary Fley, 29 Sept 1766. Hayne records

Montang, Felix Joseph & Sebina Martin, 12 Aug 1808. St. Phil
    records

Moody, Peter of Charleston, mariner, & Ann Whipple, widow,
    28 Oct 1809. (original marriage license) St. Phil records

Moody, Peter & Ann Whipple, widow, 29 Oct 1809. St. Phil
    records

Moon, Patrick & Martha Forest, ___ 1776. Hayne records

Moore, Dr. Andrew B. & ____, 29 May 1813. Sptg. Journal of the
   Ordinary 1810-1816, p. 74

Moore, James Weems Dr. of Charles Town, & Susanh. Jones of
   St. Pauls Parish, 4 Oct 1770. Hayne records

Moore, John & Sarah Fletcher, 9 June 1767. Hayne records

Moore, Joseph & Ann Taylor, widow, ___ 1777. Hayne records

Mordecai, Samuel & Cath: Andrews, 23 Dec 1778. Hayne records

Morgan, Robert & Anna Croft, colored persons, 28 Oct 1809.
   St. Phil records

Morgan, Wm. of Charles Town, & Mary Chanler, of same, 1 Jan
   1770. Hayne records

Morris, George & Cathrin White, ___ 1801(?). Cedar Springs ARP
   Records

Morris, Mark of Charles Town, & Margaret Tew, of James Island,
   14 June 1770. Hayne records

Morrow, Robert & Elis: Wood, widow, of Charles Town, 1 Nov 1778.
   Hayne records

Morrow, Wm. & Sarah Weems, 4 May 1802. Cedar Springs ARP Records

Motte, Charles of Charles Town, & Eliza: Roche, of St. Thomas
   Parish, ___ May 1768. Hayne records

Motte, Isaac of Charles Town, & Catherine Deas, of same,
   ___ 1776. Hayne records

Motte, Colo. Isaac of Charles Town, & Mary Broughton, of St.
   Johns Parish, 18 Dec 1777. Hayne records

Motte, Jacob & Ann Pickering, widow, of Charles Town, ___ June
   1763. Hayne records

Motte, James & Sylvia Mazyck, 14 April 1809. St. Phil records

Moultrie, Alexr. of Charles Town, & Charlotte Lennox, of same,
   27 May 1772. Hayne records

Moultrie, Wm., Brigr. General, & Hannah Lynch, of Charles Town,
   ___ Oct 1779. Hayne records

Moultrie, Wm. Junr. of Charles Town, & Hannah Ainslie, of St.
   Georges Parish, ___ 1776. Hayne records

Mowat, John Captn. of Charles Town, & Mary Ash, of same,
   ___ 1778. Hayne records

Muckinfus, Michael, 73, of Charles Town, & Susannah Mollson,
   51,widow, of St. Georges Parish, ___ April 1771. Hayne
   records

Muller, Albert Aerney & Magdalen Martin, ___ 1778. Hayne
   records

Mullins, George, of St. Pauls Parish, & Sarah Cattell, ___ June
   1773. Hayne records

Murray, Patrick & ___ Oats, of Charles Town, ___ 1774. Hayne records

Naisted, Frederick & Mrs. Mary Hunter, widow, 31 Aug 1809. St. Phil records

Neilson, James of Charles Town, & Hester Singletary, 30 Jan 1774. Hayne records

Neitcher(?), Richard of Chehaw & Martha Waley, of Hutsons Island, 4 April 1768. Hayne records

Netherclift, Thomas of Charles Town, & Ann McQueen of same, 22 Feb 1767. Hayne records

Nevin, Jno & Isabella Orr, 14 July 1765. Hayne records

Nevin, John, attorney of Charles Town, & Ann Baker, ___ March 1771. Hayne records

Newbery, Malachi and Ann Rowel, 18 Dec 1763. Hezekiah Smith diary

Nichau, Jacob & Esther Cromwell, 8 June 1778. Hayne records

Nichols, Samuel & Ann Ferguson, 25 June 1767. Hayne records

Nicolas, Stewart & Elis. Frederick, 1 Nov 1772. Hayne records

Nicolls, Henry of St. Pauls Parish, & Sarah Fuller, of St. Andrews Parish, ___ 1776. Hayne records

Nicolls, Richard of Charles Town, & Ann McGaw, of same, ___ Jan 1768. Hayne records

Nisbett, Wm. of Charles Town, & Jane Scott, ___ 1778. Hayne records

Norris, Andrew, of Abbeville Dist., Esqr., attorney at law, & Ann Eliza Wrainch, of Charleston, spinster, 17 June 1803. St. Phil records

North, John Laurens, atty-at-law, & Eliza Elliot Drayton, spinster, 31 Dec 1805. St. Phil records

Nurvis, John, mariner, & Ann Morris, widow, 22 March 1806. St. Phil records

Oats, Edward of Charles Town, & ___ Walker, ___ March 1767. Hayne records

Odinsell, Charles of St. Pauls Parish, & Sarah Livingston, widow, of same, 3 April 1766. Hayne records

Ohear, James of Charles Town, & Ann Gordon, of same, 10 Feb 1774. Hayne records

Oldham, Bennet of Charles Town, & Mrs. McCartey, of Beaufort, ___ Oct 1768. Hayne records

Osborne, Thos of St. Bartholomews Parish, & Catherine Spry, widow, of St. Pauls Parish, ___ May 1768. Hayne records

Oswald, Wm., planter of St. Bartholomews Parish, & Tamer Perkins, of same, 12 Nov 1771. Hayne records

Palmer, Job of Charles Town, & Sarah Morgan, 23 Oct 1774. Hayne records

Palmer, John & Ann Greaves, 21 March 1765. Hayne records

Parks, Jno. of Charleston, storekeeper, & Sarah Morgan, of St. James Santee, widow, 16 April 1803. St. Phil records

Patterson, Samuel, merchant, & Livingston Smith, spinster, 15 April 1807. St. Phil records

Pawley, Colo. Pearce of George Town, & Constant Michau, widow, ___ 1775. Hayne records

Peace, Isaac & Elis: Gibson, of Barbadoes, __ Aug 1770. Hayne records

Peak, John & Elizabeth Harvey, ___ 1778. Hayne records

Pearce, Richard, merchant of Charleston, & Harriett Petsch, 5 Jan 1813. St. Phil records

Perkins, John of Prince Williams Parish, & Sarah Cossens of Georgia, __ April 1769. Hayne records

Perry, James Dr. of St. Pauls Parish, & Frances Hunter of Charles Town, 16 Dec 1777. Hayne records

Perry, Josiah, Esqr., planter of St. Pauls & Sarah Lowndes, widow, of St. Bartholomews Parish, 17 Dec 1772. Hayne records

Perry, Joseph & Ann Stevens, ___ 1779. Hayne records

Perry, Richard of St. Pauls Parish, & Helen Hunter, of Charles Town, ___ 1778. Hayne records

Petrie, Edmond of Charles Town, & Ann Peronneau of same, 22 Aug 1779. Hayne records

Peyre, Rene, planter of St. Stevens Parish, & Elizabeth Cantey, __ March 1771. Hayne records

Piercy, Revd., of the Orphanhouse, & Cath: Elliot, of Charles Town, ___ 1776. Hayne records

Pike, Nathaniel, plaisterer, & Mary Turner, spinster, 4 Jan 1805. St. Phil records

Pillans, Doctr. Wm. & Mary Hayne, of Charles Town, 10 April 1763. Hayne records

Pincell, William & Ann Blakely, colored persons, 1 Sept 1807. St. Phil records

Pinckney, C. C., Esqr., planter & atty. of Charles Town, & Sarah Middleton, of same, 28 Sept 1773. Hayne records

Pinckney, Hobson of Charles Town, & Elizabeth Quash, of St. Thomas Parish, 22 Nov 1772. Hayne records

Pinckney, Hopson of Charles Town, & Elis: Cannon, of same, ___ 1777. Hayne records

Pinckney, Roger Esqr. of Charles Town, & Sarah Hume, widow, of St. Johns Parish, 26 March 1769. Hayne records

Pinckney, Thos Major of 1st Regt. & Elis: Moote, of Charles Town, 22 July 1779. Hayne records

Porcher, Isaac & Mary Ann Stephens, 10 May 1810. St. Phil records

Porcher, Paul Junr of St. Peters Parish, & Jane Jackson, of St. Bartholomews Parish, 6 May 1775. Hayne records

Porteous, Robert, merchant of Beaufort & Ann Wigg, of Beaufort, ___ Nov 1771. Hayne records

Postel, James Esq. of Dorchester & Elizabeth Girardeau, of St. Bartholomews Parish, ___ Dec 1766. Hayne records

Postell, James Esqr. of St. Bartholomews Parish, & Cather: Douxaint, of Charles Town, 30 Dec 1764. Hayne records

Potter, John, shoemaker, of Charles Town, & Sarah Hinds, of same, ___ Jan 1771. Hayne records

Powell, Dr. John of St. Helena & Martha Meggett of same, 3 Sept 1765. Hayne records

Powell, Robt. Wm. of Charles Town, & Alice Hopton, 11 Jan 1774. Hayne records

Powell, Thos., printer of Charles Town, & Mary Brown, of same, 3 Nov 1773. Hayne records

Poyas, Jno Ernest of Charles Town, & Mary Schwartzkop, widow, of same, ___ 1776. Hayne records

Presly, John & Marg't Patterson, 15 Nov 1798. Cedar Springs ARP Records

Presly, Robt. & Eliz. Clark, 13 Dec 1809. Cedar Springs ARP Records

Price, Daniel & Eleanor Jones, ___ April 1767. Hayne records

Price, Wm., merchant of Charles Town, & Ann Nicholls, widow, of same, 13 May 1772. Hayne records

Prince, John & Elizabeth Bond Buonetheau, 5 March 1809. St. Phil records

Pringle, James Reid, atty-at-law, & Elizabeth Mary McPherson, spinster, 19 March 1807. St. Phil records

Prioleau, Hext of Charles Town, & Margt. Williams of same, 9 March 1775. Hayne records

Prioleau, John of Prince Williams Parish, & Jane Broadbelt, of same, ___ 1774. Hayne records

Prioleau, Samuel Junr. of Charles Town, & Catherine Gordon, of St. Johns Parish, 9 Oct 1766. Hayne records

Pritchard, Paul Jr. of Charleston, shipwright, & Catharine Hamilton, of same, spinster, 10 Feb 1803. St. Phil records

Proctor, Richard, planter of St. Helenas Parish, & Ann Vinson, of St. Bartholomews Parish, __ Oct 1772. Hayne records

Purcell, William & Ann Blakely, 1 Sept 1807. St. Phil records

Purvis, Jno of Ninety Six, & Ann Pritchard, of Orangeburgh, __ 1775. Hayne records

Quelch, Andw. Capt. & Sarah Fyffe, widow, ___ 1779. Hayne records

Ramadge, Charles of Charles Town, & Frances Swallow, widow, of same, 28 June 1774. Hayne records

Ramsey, Dr. David of Charles Town, & Sabina Ellis, of same, 9 Feb 1775. Hayne records

Rantowle, Alexr. & Eleanor Rantowle, ___ 1778. Hayne records

Rantowle, James of Charles Town, & Elisabeth Ives, ___ 1774. Hayne records

Rayer, Henry, shopkeeper, & Anne Labar, widow, 15 Jan 1805. St. Phil records

Redley, John & ___ Quince, black people, 27 May 1806. St. Phil records

Reid, Andrew, rope maker of Charles Town, & Eliza: Sarrazin of same, 5 May 1765. Hayne records

Reilly, John, of Savannah, & Mary Tucker, of Charleston, colored, 7 May 1807. St. Phil records

Remington, Jno Junr. of Charles Town, & Sarah Donavan, of same, 6 April 1774. Hayne records

Remington, Dr. Wm. of Edisto & Ann Eaton, of same, 14 May 1769. Hayne records

Reuty(?), John & Nancy Himely, 11 June 1806(?), at St. Michaels. St. Phil records

Reynolds, Benjn. & Sarah Smelie, widow, __ April 1774. Hayne records

Rhind, David of Charles Town, & Elis: Cleiland, of same, 22 Dec 1774. Hayne records

Richardson, Capt. Edward & Rachel Heatly, of St. Mathews Parish, ___ 1776. Hayne records

Richardson, Jno. of St. Augustine & Amy Welchuysen, of Charles Town, 27 March 1768. Hayne records

Richardson, Wm. of Charles Town, & Ann Guignard, 11 Oct 1768. Hayne records

Rivell, George of Charleston, mercht., & Margt. Timmons, of same, spinster. 10 April 1803. St. Phil records

Rivers, Nehemiah of James Island & Bulah Law, __ Nov 1768.
Hayne records

Rivers, Robt. & Ann Hunscombe, of Johns Island, ___ 1777.
Hayne records

Rivers, Thomas of James Island, & Margaret Warham, of Charles
Town, 27 Aug 1778. Hayne records

Roach, Wm. & Mary Campbell, of Christ Church Parish, ___ 1778.
Hayne records

Robert, John of Indian Land, & Elizabeth Dixon, __ May 1770.
Hayne records

Roberts, Robert, army artillery lt., & Harriet Halteisen Mercer,
spinster, 10 July 1806. St. Phil records

Robnett, Jno & Margaret Neisbett, marriage license directed to
Rev. James Templeton, 27 Jan 1801. Spartanburg Journal of
Ordinary, p. 6

Roche, Francis of St. Thomas Parish, & Mary Jennings, __ May
1768. Hayne records

Roche, Thomas of St. Thomas Parish, & Ann Marion, 31 Dec 1778.
Hayne records

Rogers, Noah & Mary Covan, 25 Oct 1803; Daniel Morrow, bondsman;
Wm. Hemingway, wit; license directed to the Revd. William
Holt. Horry MB

Roper, Benj. Dart, planter, & Barbara Calder Jenkins, dau.
Micah Jenkins, 26 Feb 1807. St. Phil records

Roper, William Esqr., attorney of Charles Town, & Hannah Dart,
of same, 5 May 1771. Hayne records

Rose, Alexr. of Charles Town, & Margt. Smith, of New York, 21
Jan 1779. Hayne records

Rose, Francis, of St. Andrews Parish, & Eliz: Linning of
Charles Town, 3 July 1767. Hayne records

Rose, Jeremiah & Susannah Stent, ___ 1779. Hayne records

Rose, John & Susannah I'on, ___ 1778. Hayne records

Rose, Robert of St. Andrews Parish, & Rebecca Rivers, of same,
10 May 1770. Hayne records

Rose, Thos of St. Andrews Parish, & Mary Ann Clerk Sanders, of
St. Pauls Parish, 26 May 1770. Hayne records

Rose, Thomas of St. Andrews Parish, & Mary Blake, of Charles
Town, ___ 1774. Hayne records

Rosse, John & Eliz M'Gilvray, widow, of Charles Town, __ Jan
1765 or 1766(?). Hayne records

Roulain, James & Angelica Varambaut, widow, 18 July 1768. Hayne
records

Rout, George & Ann Parker, widow, ___ 1778. Hayne records

SUPPLEMENT TO SOUTH CAROLINA MARRIAGES 1688-1820

Rowand, Robert of Charles Town, & Mary McKewn, of St. Pauls
Parish, 12 Sept 1765. Hayne records

Rowe, Charles Christopher, Colo, of Orangeburg & ___ Chevillette,
widow, of same, __ July 1771. Hayne records

Royal, Wm. of James Island, & Martha Samways, ___ 1779. Hayne
records

Ruberry, John & Elis. Wilkie, 1 Nov 1772. Hayne records

Rudhall, Willm. of Charles Town, & Mary Miller, ___ 1777. Hayne
records

Rugely, Rowland of Charles Town, & Hamilton Dawson, 16 or 18
March 1775. Hayne records

Rutledge, Andw of Charles Town & Elis Gadsden, of same, 24 Sept
1767. Hayne records

Rutledge, Edward of Charles Town, & Harriet Middleton, of same,
1 March 1774. Hayne records

Rutledge, John & Eliza Grimke, of Charles Town, 1 May 1763.
Hayne records

Sanders, Roger Parker of St. Pauls Parish, & Amarinthia Lowndes
of Charles Town, 26 Sept 1776. Hayne records

Sarazin, Jonathan of Charles Town, & Sarah Prioleau, widow, of
same, 22 June 1770. Hayne records

Sasportassa, Abraham of Charles Town, & Rebecca Dacosta, of
same, 16 Sept 1778. Hayne records

Saunders, John of St. Bartholomews Parish, & Elizabeth Palmer,
of same, 26 April 1770. Hayne records

Saunders, John & Martha Hunt, widow, ___ 1777. Hayne records

Saunders, William of St. Bartholomews Parish, & Eliza: Saunders
of same, __ June 1770. Hayne records

Saunds, James of Charles Town, & Hannah Dewick, of Dorchester,
4 Dec 1767. Hayne records

Savage, John, of Ninety Six, & Ann Gaillard, __ Feb 1769.
Hayne records

Savage, Thos of Charles Town, & Mary Butler, of Georgia, 21 April
1767. Hayne records

Sawyer, Elisha of the West Indies & Ann Blake, of Charles Town,
___ 1777. Hayne records

Schermerhorn, Cornelius & Caroline Snyder, of Charles Town, 20
Aug 1778. Hayne records

Scott, John of Charles Town, & Sar: Perronneau, of same, __ Dec
1768. Hayne records

Scott, Joseph, aged 18, of Edisto, & Catherine Adams, aged 12,
of same, ___ 1774. Hayne records

Scott, William of St. Andrews Parish & Sarah Brailsford, of St. Georges Parish, 17 Oct 1765. Hayne records

Scott, William Junr., merchant of Charles Town, & Elizabeth Legare, of same, 2 April 1771. Hayne records

Scott, Wm. Junr. of Charles Town, & Jane Bruce, of Christ Church Parish, 19 March 1776. Hayne records

Scott, Wm. Junr. of Charles Town, & Elis: Rivers, of James Island, 22 Dec 1778. Hayne records

Scott, William Morgan, of Charleston, merchant, & Margaret Holmes, of same, widow, 30 Sept 1811. (original marriage license) St. Phil records

Screven, John, planter of James Island & Patience Holmes, of Johns Island, __ Feb 1772. Hayne records

Screven, Thomas & Eleanor Hart, __ March 1770. Hayne records

Seabrook, Benjn. & Sarah Calder, of Edisto, 1 May 1767. Hayne records

Seaver, Abraham & Hannah M'Grath, 20 Dec 1778. Hayne records

Seemerhorn, Arnout & Mary Mackey, widow, 23 Feb 1769. Hayne records

Sexias, Abram Mendas & Ricksy Hart, of Charles Town, __ 1777. Hayne records

Shackleford, Wm. F., of Georgetown, attorney, & Miss Eliza Ashby, of St. Thomas parish, spinster, 15 Dec 1803. St. Phil records

Sharpless, John of St. Bartholomews Parish, & Ann Sleigh of same, 17 July 1766. Hayne records

Shaw, Edward & Peggy Matthews, 9 June 1808. St. Phil records

Shepheard, Charles of Charles Town, & Eliz: Radcliffe of Charles Town, __ Feb 1768. Hayne records

Shepheard, Charles of St. Bartholomews Parish, & Elisabeth Gibbes, of Charles Town, 27 Aug 1775. Hayne records

Shepherd, Wm. & Elis. Steel, ___ 1770. Hayne records

Shubrick, Richard, planter of St. Pauls Parish, & Susannah Bulline, of Goosecreek, 1 Oct 1772. Hayne records

Shubrick, Thos. Capt. of 5th Regt., & Mary Branford, of St. Pauls Parish, ___ 1778. Hayne records

Simmons, Charles & Mary Miller, 18 March 1779. Hayne records

Simmons, John of Prince Williams Parish, & Susannah Hayne, of St. Pauls Parish, 21 May 1776. Hayne records

Simons, Charles Dewar & Sarah Barksdale, 22 Sept 1807. St. Phil records

Simons, Edward of Charles Town, & Lidia Ball, of Goose creek, 18 Oct 1771. Hayne records

Simons, Edward, Esqr., planter, & Mary Simons, of Thos. Simons, decd., 27 Nov 1811. St. Phil records

Simons, Edward & Mary Read Simons, 27 Nov 1810. St. Phil records

Simons, James Dewar, & Harleston Corbett, dau. of Thomas Corbett Sen., Esquire, m. by Rev. Dr. Jenkins, 22 Jan 1807. St. Phil records

Simons, Keathing of Charles Town, & Sarah Lewis, of Goosecreek, 9 June 1774. Hayne records

Simons, Maurice, of Charles Town, & Mary Mitchel, of Prince George Parish, 19 July 1764. Hayne records

Simons, Peter & St. James Parish, & Mary Greenland, __ Dec 1770. Hayne records

Simpson, John of Charleston, mercht., & Mary Godfrey, spinster, 1 Jan 1804. St. Phil records

Simpson, John of Georgia, & Elizabeth Dale, of South Carolina, __ March 1770. Hayne records

Simpson, Jno. Esqr., planter of Georgia, & Ann McKensie, of Savannah, __ July 1772. Hayne records

Simpson, William & Catharine Devall, spinster, 10 Nov 1807. St. Phil records

Singellton, John & Jane Miller, ___ 1779. Hayne records

Singellton, John Junr. of St. Bartholomews Parish, & Dorothy Johnson, of Peedee, 2 Dec 1779. Hayne records

Singellton, Richard of St. Bartholomews Parish, & Margt. Darquier of same, 13 Oct 1777. Hayne records

Singelton, Daniel of St. Bartholomews Parish, & Ann Bowler, of same, 7 March 1774. Hayne records

Singleton, Benjn., planter, & Elizabeth St. John, both of St. Bartholomews Parish, 10 Dec 1764. Hayne records

Sinkler, William & Miss Eliza Broun, 16 Jan 1810. St. Phil records

Skirving, James Esqr. of Charles Town, & Charl: Mathewes, widow, of same, 18 March 1769. Hayne records

Skirving, James Junr. of St. Bartholomews Parish, & Sarah Vinson, of same, 16 Jan 1766. Hayne records

Skirving, Wm of St. Bartholomews Parish, & Mary Shehevral, of St. Pauls Parish, 10 April 1766. Hayne records

Skirving, William of St. Pauls Parish, & Anne Holland Hutchinson, of St. Bartholomews Parish, 12 Jan 1769. Hayne records

Skottowe, Thos & Lucia Bellinger, 30 Dec 1766. Hayne records

Slann, Joseph, planter of Slanns Island, & Jane Baron, of St. Pauls Parish, __ May 1772. Hayne records

Slappy, John George of Camden Dist., & Christina Spyinger, widow,
27 May 1782; George Slappy, Frederick Spyinger, trustees;
Christian Theus, Thomas Heath, Cunrod Mires, wit. Misc Rec
UU, pp. 137-140

Smith, Archar, of Charles Town, & Florence Waring, of St.
Georges Parish, __ March 1776. Hayne records

Smith, Archibald Jr. of Charleston, gent., & Ann Chivers, of
same, widow, 10 March 1803. St. Phil records

Smith, Benjn., planter of Goosecreek, & Cather: Ball, of St.
Johns Parish, __ April 1773. Hayne records

Smith, Benj. of Goosecreek & Sarah Smith, of Charles Town,
__ 1775. Hayne records

Smith, Benjn. of Charles Town, & Sarah Dry, of North Carolina,
__ 1777. Hayne records

Smith, Charles of St. Bartholomews Parish, & Mary Blinco, of
same, 2 July 1772. Hayne records

Smith, Francis of St. Bartholomews Parish, & Sarah Hull, 28
April 1774. Hayne records

Smith, Henry of Goose Creek & Elis: Ball of St. John's Parish,
13 Dec 1764. Hayne records

Smith, James, merchant of Charles Town, & Ann Thomas of St.
Thomas Parish, 18 March 1773. Hayne records

Smith, John, merchant of Charles Town, & Susan Richardson, of
same, __ April 1772. Hayne records

Smith, Joseph of New York & Elis: Gordon of Charles Town, __ Oct
1770. Hayne records

Smith, Josiah of Charleston, mariner, & Sophia Smith, of same,
spinster, 10 Dec 1803. St. Phil records

Smith, Nicolas, Goldsmith of Charles Town, & Mary Cripps, widow,
8 Aug 1778. Hayne records

Smith, Peter of Charles Town, & Mary Middleton, of same, __ Nov
1776. Hayne records

Smith, Phil Esqr. of St. Bartholomews Parish, & Eliza: Stobo,
widow, of St. Pauls Parish, 17 April 1766. Hayne records

Smith, Press of Charles Town, & Elis: Miles of St. Pauls
Parish, __ Oct 1776. Hayne records

Smith, Robt. Revd. of St. Philips Parish, & Sarah Shubrick, of
Charles Town, 17 Feb 1774. Hayne records

Smith, Roger of Charles Town, & Mary Rutledge, of same, 7 April
1768. Hayne records

Smith, Thomas of St. Bartholomews Parish, & Hannah Cockran, of
Chehaws, 22 March 1769. Hayne records

Smith, Thomas of St. Bartholomews Parish, & Jane Young, of
Charles Town, 11 Nov 1777. Hayne records

Smith, Thomas of St. Bartholomews Parish, & Hannah Cochran, of same, 19 April 1770. Hayne records

Smith, Thos Loughton, & Elliz Inglis, of Charles Town, 29 May 1763. Hayne records

Smith, William, planter, & Elizabeth Dalton, of St. Bartholomew's Parish, 23 Feb 1765. Hayne records

Snow, Chester Francis Cleveland, & Esther Astuin, 20 Dec 1808. St. Phil records

Somers, Jno. Capt., planter of St. Pauls Parish, & Martha Roper, of Charles Town, 22 June 1772. Hayne records

Somers, Peter & Phoebe Watson, blacks, 13 June 1806. St. Phil records

Somersall, Wm. of St. Christo & Sarah Legare of Charles Town, 11 Dec 1766. Hayne records

Somersall, Wm. of Charles Town, & Sarah Crostwaite, widow, of Prince Williams Parish, ___ 1774. Hayne records

Sommers, Captn. Jno. of St. Pauls Parish, & Martha Perry, of same, ___ 1774. Hayne records

Spence, Peter, Dr. of Jacksonburg & Frances Brown of George Town, 7 April 1771. Hayne records

Splatt, Edward of St. Pauls Parish, & Esther Dean of same, 24 July 1766. Hayne records

Spry, Joseph of St. Pauls Parish, & Cather: Tookerman, of St. Bartholomews Parish, 29 May 1766. Hayne records

St. John, Audeon, planter, & Mary Law, widow of St. Bartholomews Parish, 31 Oct 1771. Hayne records

St. John, James of Charles Town, & Eliza: Boomer, of same, ___ March 1770. Hayne records

Stacey, Edward of St. Bartholomews Parish, & Hester Little, of same, 24 April 1774. Hayne records

Stanyarne, James of Jno Island, & Henrietta Raven, widow, 30 Oct 1767. Hayne records

Stanyarne, James, planter of St. Pauls Parish, & Susannah Scott, of St. Andrews Parish, 25 June 1772. Hayne records

Stanyarne, Joseph, planter of St. Pauls Parish, & Mary Hartley, widow of St. Pauls Parish, 9 Dec 1773. Hayne records

Stent, Saml. & Rachel Rivers, ___ Dec 1772. Hayne records

Stephen & Ann (Crowly), 23 April 1808. St. Phil records

Stevens, Daniel of Charles Town, & Patience Norton, of same, 6 Dec 1767. Hayne records

Stevens, Daniel of Charles Town, & Mary Adams, widow, of Port Royal, ___ April 1779. Hayne records

Stevens, Jacob Junr. of St. Bartholomews Parish, & Mary Gough, of same, 3 July 1766. Hayne records

Stevens, Jervis Henry of Charles Town, & Elisabeth Davis, __ Dec 1775. Hayne records

Stevens, Richard, planter of Beaufort & Mary Smith, of same, 18 Dec 1765. Hayne records

Stevenson, Hamilton & J___ Murray, ___ 1775. Hayne records

Stevenson, Jas. & Fanny Weems, 9 July 1799. Cedar Springs ARP Records

Stevenson, James & Elis: Eccles, widow, of St. George Parish, 14 Aug 1774. Hayne records

Stevenson, Peter, planter of Charles Town, & Mary Jones Snelling, of same, 7 Jan 1773. Hayne records

Steward, Chas. August:, Capt. Regt., & Sarah Powell, of Pedee River, 15 June 1769. Hayne records

Stock, Gabriel & Ann Hampton, of St. Bartholomews Parish, 3 Dec 1766. Hayne records

Stocks, John of St. Bartholomews Parish, & Margaret Young, of Charles Town, 10 Nov 1778. Hayne records

Stone, Benj. Capt. of James Island, & Love Rivers, ___ 1779. Hayne records

Stone, Samuel & Catherine Washington, 30 Aug 1818; Terry Cockerell, Robert Knox, trustees; Reuben Pickett, Micajah Pickett, wit. Fairfield Deed Book BB, pp. 148-149

Streight, Christ: Revd., of Charles Town, & Mary Hoof, 23 July 1778. Hayne records

Strickland, Jas., Innskeeper of Charles Town, & Elisabeth Hennington, of same, 30 Aug 1772. Hayne records

Stuart, Revd. Jas. of Prince George, & Ann Waties, widow, __ Sept 1773. Hayne records

Sullivan, Philip Capt. & Susannah Shackleford, ___ 1778. Hayne records

Sullivan, Timothy, merchant, & Mary Hamilton, spinster, 20 Feb 1806. St. Phil records

Sutton, Robt. & Margt. Guerry, of St. Thomas Parish, ___ 1775. Hayne records

Swadler, George, planter of St. Bartholomews Parish, & Mary Balfour, widow, of Charles Town, __ June 1773. Hayne records

Swainston, Robt of Watbro & Deborah Sabb, of St. Thos Parish, 15 Feb 1767. Hayne records

Swallow, William, merchant of Charles Town, & Sarah Prince, 26 Oct 1771. Hayne records

Sweeny, James, of Charleston, vendue master, & Eliza Gray, of same, widow, 1 May 1803. St. Phil records

Swinton, William of St. Pauls Parish, & Sarah Baron, widow of
St. Bartholomews Parish, 12 June 1766. Hayne records

Taggart, Wm., Lt. 3d Regt., & Mary Haly, widow, of Hamstead,
___ 1778. Hayne records

Talor, Barnet & Mary Lennox, __ Dec 1771. Hayne records

Tart, Nathan, planter, of Christ Church Parish, & Frances
Garden, of St. Thomas Parish, __ April 1771. Hayne records

Taylor, Charles, mariner, & Sophia George, spinster, 9 April
1805. St. Phil records

Taylor, James, B. binder, of Charles Town, & Ann Chopard, of
Charles Town, 1 Oct 1770. Hayne records

Taylor, Joseph, ship carpenter, & Mary Willis, widow, 25 Nov
1806, by Rev. N. Bowen. St. Phil records

Taylor, Paul & Martha Miller, ___ 1778. Hayne records

Telfair, William, of Georgia, & Elisa: Bellinger, of St.
Andrews Parish, 21 March 1769.

Theus, Jno. of John's Island & ___ Simmons, widow of same,
__ May 1765. Hayne records

Thomas, Edward of St. Johns Parish, & Ann Gibbes of Charles
Town, 29 Sept 1767. Hayne records

Thomson, Jas. Hamden of Charles Town, & Eliz. Mary Trezevant of
same, ___ 1775. Hayne records

Thomas, Revd. Jno of Charles Town, & Mary Lamboll, of same,
__ Feb 1768. Hayne records

Thomas, Saml. & Jane Douxsaint, of Charles Town, 30 Oct 1768.
Hayne records

Thompson, Hugh of St. Bartholomews Parish, & Mary Penny, widow,
of same, 29 March 1767. Hayne records

Thompson, John of St. Bartholomew's Parish, & Johanna Kilvart,
10 April 1765. Hayne records

Thomson, George of Charles Town, & Jean Yorston, of Scotland,
___ 1767. Hayne records

Tiddyman, Philip, Silver smith of Charles Town, & Esther Rose,
of same, 13 Oct 1772. Hayne records

Tilghman, Gideon of St. Bartholomews Parish, & Mary Pounds,
4 May 1774. Hayne records

Tilly, William & Martha Willson, 19 April 1804; John Willson,
bondsman; license directed to Revd. Mr. Hugh Porter; Wm.
Hemingway, wit. Horry MB

Timmons, Thomas of St. Bartholomew's Parish, & Susanna Timmons,
of same, 2 Dec 1765. Hayne records

Tims, Thomas & Ann Hext, ___ 1779. Hayne records

Tobias, Jacob of Charles Town, & Rachel Dacosta of same, __ 1775. Hayne records

Todd, Richard & Elis: Winborn, __ Jan 1769. Hayne records

Tonge, Revd. Jno. of St. Pauls Parish, & Susan: Perry, of St. Pauls Parish, 5 Sept 1768. Hayne records

Toomer, Anthony of Charles Town, & Ann Warham, of same, 2 Aug 1767. Hayne records

Toomer, Benjn. & Mary Nichols, 10 June 1767. Hayne records

Toussiger, James & Margt. Ball, __ 1777. Hayne records

Trapier, Paul Esqr. of George Town, & Mrs. Waties, __ June 1769. Hayne records

Trapier, Paul Junr., planter of Geo Town, & Elizabeth Foissin, of Charles Town, __ Nov 1771. Hayne records

Trescot, Edward of Charles Town, & Cath: Bouquet, of same, __ 1777. Hayne records

Troup, John & Frances Gordon, of Charles Town, 30 May 1763. Hayne records

Trusler, Wm. of Charles Town, & Jane Anderson, of same, 31 Dec 1778. Hayne records

Tucker, Benj. Capt. & Sarah Balantine, 22 Dec 1778. Hayne records

Tucker, Danl. of George Town, & Elis: Hyrne, of Charles Town, __ 1779. Hayne records

Tucker, Thos Capt. of Charles Town, & Mary Flin, widow of George Town, __ 1775. Hayne records

Tucker, Thos Tudor, Dr. of Charles Town, & Esther Evans of St. George Parish, 30 June 1774. Hayne records

Turpin, Joseph of Charles Town, & Hannah Caskin, of same, __ May 1772. Hayne records

Valk, Jacob of Charles Town, & Ann Roberts, widow, of same, __ 1778. Hayne records

Valton, Peter of Charles Town, & Eliz. Timothy, of same, 3 Nov 1767. Hayne records

Vanderhorst, Arnoldus, Esqr. of Christ Church Parish, & Elizabeth Raven, of Charles Town, 5 March 1771. Hayne records

Vanderhorst, Elias & Mary Cooper, of Charles Town, 12 July 1763. Hayne records

Varambaut, Frances of Charles Town, & Angelica La Tour, of same, 27 July 1767. Hayne records

Vardell, Turner & Elis: Tucker, __ April 1769. Hayne records

SUPPLEMENT TO SOUTH CAROLINA MARRIAGES 1688-1820

Vaux, Percival Edward, planter, & Sarah Richards, spinster, 19
   Dec 1805. St. Phil records

Vaux, Wm., of George Town, & Ann Pawley, of Waccamaw, __ Feb
   1778. Hayne records

Villepontoux, Benjn. of Charles Town, & Jane Dupont of St.
   Peters Parish, 1 April 1766. Hayne records

Wadingham, Samuel of St. Bartholomews Parish, & Rebecca
   Shoemaker, of same, 28 Oct 1766. Hayne records

Wainwright, Richd. of Charles Town, & Ann Dewar, __ Dec 1776.
   Hayne records

Wakefield, James, merchant of Charles Town, & Sarah Cannon, of
   Charles Town, 26 Nov 1771. Hayne records

Walker, Alexr of Charles Town, & Ann Fairchild, of St. Paul's
   Parish, __ June 1765. Hayne records

Walter, Jno Allen, of Ashley River, & Jane Oliphant, of Charles
   Town, ___ 1774. Hayne records

Walter, Paul of Charles Town, & Ann Geigleman, of St.
   Bartholomews Parish, ___ 1778. Hayne records

Walter, Richard, merchant of Dorchester, & Harriet Cantey, of
   Christ Church Parish, 2 May 1765. Hayne records

Walter, Richard Charles of Statesburg, & Mary Ford, daughter of
   George Gord, 15 May 1797; William James of Stateburgh,
   trustee; Sarah Hendlin, Thos Eveleigh, wit. Misc Rec B,
   pp. 391-395

Walter, Thomas of Charles Town, & Ann Lesesne of Daniels Island,
   26 March 1769. Hayne records

Warby, William K., M. D., & Mary M. Wilson, 14 April 1810.
   St. Phil records

Waring, Benjamin, Esq., planter, of St. George's Parish, & Ann
   Waring, of same, 18 April 1756. Hayne records

Waring, John of Charles Town, & Charlotte Williamson, widow, of
   same, 16 Sept 1770. Hayne records

Waring, John of Charles Town, & Mary Hamlin, widow, of
   Dorchester, ___ 1779. Hayne records

Waring, Jno. Junr. of St. Georges Parish, & Ann Smith, of St.
   Johns Parish, ___ 1778. Hayne records

Waring, Joseph of St. Georges Parish, & Mary Ioor, of same,
   __ March 1778. Hayne records

Waring, Morton of St. Georges Parish, & Edith Waring, of
   Dorchester, ___ 1777. Hayne records

Waring, Richard of St. Georges Parish, & Ann Branford, of St.
   James Parish, __ Nov 1768. Hayne records

Waring, Thomas, merchant of Charles Town, & Mary Waring of St.
   George's Parish, 13 June 1765. Hayne records

Waring, Thomas of St. Georges Parish, & Martha Waring, of same, __ May 1778. Hayne records

Watts, Robt & Jane Ferguson, 21 Nov 1765. Hayne records

Wayne, Richard of Charles Town, & Eliza: Clifford, of St. Bartholomews Parish, 14 Sept 1769. Hayne records

Wayne, Wm. of Charles Town, & Esther Trezevant of same, 8 May 1777. Hayne records

Webb, Benjn. of St. Bartholomews Parish, & Ann Doyley of Charles Town, 14 March 1775. Hayne records

Webb, Benjamin & Chloe Webb, blacks, 13 June 1806. St. Phil records

Webb, David Cannon, merchant, & Eliza Ann Ladson, spinster, 28 Nov 1805. St. Phil records

Webb, John of Charles Town, & Mary Doughty, of same, __ Jan 1769. Hayne records

Webb, William of St. Bartholomews Parish, & Margt. Doyley, of Charles Town, ___ 1774. Hayne records

Webber, Wm, overseer of St. Bartholomew's Parish, & Sarah Smith, 5 Dec 1765. Hayne records

Webster, Henry of Jacksonburg, & Susanna Ford, widow of Round O, 18 May 1769. Hayne records

Weems, James & Agness Gray, 18 Dec 1800. Cedar Springs ARP Records

Weir, James & Elis: Baird, ___ 1776. Hayne records

Welch, Henry & Mary Brenan, widow, ___ 1778. Hayne records

Wells, Edgar & Caludia Bennet, ___ 1779. Hayne records

Wells, Dr. John, of Johns Island, & Mary Winburn, of same, __ Dec 1772. Hayne records

Welsman, James, pilot, & Amelia Holwell, spinster, 22 Nov 1807. St. Phil records

Wesner, Frederick & Elizabeth Abel Reeve, 18 April 1811. St. Phil records

Weston, Plowden of Charles Town, & Mary Ann Mazyck of same, __ March 1775. Hayne records

Whaley, James, of St. Bartholomews Parish, & Sarah Denny, 7 Sept 1766. Hayne records

Whitaker, Richard & Frances Kaen, widow, 13 Dec 1807. St. Phil records

White, Andw & Lucy Morris, 30 March 1802. Cedar Springs ARP Records

White, Blake Leay, carpenter of Charles Town, & Elisabeth Bourquin, 7 April 1772. Hayne records

White, John M. & Rebecca Hardy, 22 March 1808.   St. Phil records

White, Thomas of St. Bartholomews Parish, & Rebecca Harden, of
    St. Bartholomews Parish, 15 April 1767.   Hayne records

White, Wm. of St. Johns Parish, planter, & Miss Ann Maronett,
    of Charleston, spinster, 17 May 1803.   St. Phil records

Whiting, John, turner, & Jane Willis, spinster, 10 May 1806.
    St. Phil records

Wigfall, Benjamin, planter of St. Thomas Parish, & Martha
    Dutarq, 1 Aug 1771.   Hayne records

Wigfall, Joseph of Christ Church Parish, & Sarah Shackleford,
    widow, 21 Jan 1779.   Hayne records

Wigg, Wm Hazard, planter of St. Helenas Parish, & Esther Hutson,
    of St. Bartholomews Parish, 11 May 1773.   Hayne records

Wilkie, John & Jane Hext, widow, of Edisto, __ Oct 1770.   Hayne
    records

Wilkinson, Wm. of St. Pauls Parish, & Margt. Wilkinson, of same,
    ____ 1779.   Hayne records

William & Clarissa (Mey), 26 April 1808.   St. Phil records

Williams, Jas. Green & Elis: Tomlinson, widow, of Johns Island,
    25 Jan 1774.   Hayne records

Williams, Robt Junr., attorney of Charles Town, & Ann Roper, of
    same, 7 Feb 1771.   Hayne records

Williamson, John & Ann Williams, 26 Dec 1807.   St. Phil records

Williamson, Richard, planter, of St. Pauls Parish, & Tobitha
    Eddings of same, 23 April 1765.   Hayne records

Willply, Dr. Benj. of Combahee & Sarah McGaw of Charles Town,
    __ July 1771.   Hayne records

Wilson, George & Susana Anderson, __ Nov 1801.   Cedar Springs
    ARP Records

Wilson, Jas. & Jane Morrow, 7 July 1803.   Cedar Springs ARP
    Records

Wilson, Jehu, planter of St. Pauls & Ann Stevens, widow of St.
    Bartholomews Parish, __ Sept 1773.   Hayne records

Wilson, John & Mary Rivers, 14 Dec 1769.   Hayne records

Wilson, John, merchant of Charles Town, & Mary Bonneau, of
    same, 12 Oct 1773.   Hayne records

Wilson, Jno., aged 20½ of Edisto, & Mary Rake, widow, aged 79½
    of same, 7 Sept 1774.   Hayne records

Wilson, John & Margt. Hazell, __ June 1777.   Hayne records

Wilson, Jno. Capt. of St. Pauls Parish, & Mary Ladson, widow,
    of Johns Island, 2 Sept 1779.   Hayne records

Wilson, Wm., merchant of Charles Town, & Mary Hervey, of same, __ Jan 1772. Hayne records

Winchester, Jonathan of Charleston, house carpenter, & Mary Parker, of same, widow, 8 June 1803. St. Phil records

Wise, Major Saml. of 3d Regt. & Ann Beattie, widow, of St. Bartholomews Parish, ___ 1778. Hayne records

Withers, John & Frances Gray, ___ 1777. Hayne records

Withers, Thomas & ___ Deveaux, widow, ___ 1778. Hayne records

Wood, Joseph & Mary Sullivan, 30 April 1766. Hayne records

Woodberry, Jno., merchant of Charles Town, & Sarah Anderson, 14 May 1772. Hayne records

Woodcraft, Richard of St. Bartholomews Parish, & Rizpah Rivers, of St. Andrews Parish, 27 Aug 1778. Hayne records

Wragg, William Esqr. of Charles Town, & Henrietta Wragg, of same, 5 Feb 1769. Hayne records

Wright, Alexander of Georgia, & Eliz. Izzard, of Goosecreek, 6 April 1769. Hayne records

Yeomans, Thomas & Dorcas Fendin, 10 April 1765. Hayne records

Broun, Eliza 37
Brown, Ann 10
  Frances 39
  Margaret 11
  Margt 6
  Mary 6, 32
Bruce, Jane 36
Bruton, Catharine 14
  John 14
Buchannan, Sarah 2
Bulline, Susannah 22, 36
Buonetheau, Elizabeth Bond 32
Burns, Ann 19
Burrows, Mary 2
Butler, Mary 35
Cahusac, Sarah 15
Calder, Sarah 36
Campbell, Elizabeth (Mrs.) 17
  Helen 14
  Mary 34
Cannon, Elis. 32
  Lucy 15
  Sarah 43
Cantey, Elizabeth 31
  Harriet 43
  Sarah 7
Cantle, Elis. (Mrs.) 1
Canty, Mary 23
Carroll, Henrietta 27
Cart, Harriott Ann 16
Carter, Mary 6
Caskin, Hannah 42
Cattell, Sarah 29
Caunou, Venus 11
Chandler, Rachel 9
  Sarah White 25
Chanler, Mary 29
  Susanh. 17
Cheesborough, Elis. 19
Chevillette, (?) 35
Chicken, Cath. 11
Chiffelle, Christian 11
Chilcotte, (?) (Mrs.) 26
Chisolm, Christiana 7
Chivers, Ann (Mrs.) 38
Chopard, Ann 41
Christie, Elis. 18
  Sarah 22
Clark, Ann 16
  Eliz. 32
Cleator, Cath. 5
  Elisabeth (Mrs.) 4
Cleiland, Elis. 33
  Sarah 2
Clement, Amelia 13
Clifford, Eliza. 44
  Jane 3
Coachman, Elis. 27
  Mary 1
  Sarah 12
Cobie, Michael 16
  Susannah (Mrs.) 16
Cochran, Agness 26
  Hannah 39
  Jane 9

Cochran (cont.)
  Margt. (Mrs.) 10
  Mary Eugenia 2
Cockerell, Terry 40
Cockran, Hannah 38
Coggeshall, James 16
Colcock, Mary 7
Cole, Mary 23
Colles, Mary 2
Colleton, Jane (Lady) 16
Collins, Charlotte 8
Collis, Eliz. 19
Connely, Mary Haley 8
Cook, Margt (Mrs.) 3
  Mary 2
Cooper, George 28
  James 9
  Mary 42
Corbett, Harleston 37
  Thomas (Sr.) 37
Cossens, Mary 3
  Sarah 31
Cotton, (?) 18
Couturier, Henrietta 9
Covan, Mary 34
Cox, Alice 24
  Richard 14
Cripps, Elizabeth 13
  Mary (Mrs.) 16, 38
Croft, Anna 29
Cromwell, Esther 30
Crook, Joanna 2
Crostwaite, Sarah (Mrs.) 39
Crowly, Ann 39
Crowson, Jacob 22
  Mary Ann 22
Cummings, Elis. 18
Cuthbert, Mary (Mrs.) 13
Dacosta, Rachel 42
  Rebecca 35
  Sarah 27
Dale, Elizabeth 37
  Rebecca 9
Dalton, Elizabeth 39
Dandridge, Frances (Mrs.) 20
Danford, Mary 24
Daniel, Elis. 24
  Mary 2
Daniell, Lewis 22
Darquier, Margt. 37
Dart, Ann 25
  Hannah 34
Davis, Elisabeth 40
  Frances 17
  Walne 15
Davison, J. 25
Dawson, Hamilton 35
De St. Julien, Judith 17
Dean, Esther 39
Deas, Catherine 29
  Elis. 28
  Mary 21
Delancy, Alice 21
Delka, Cath. 6
Denny, Sarah 44

Devall, Catharine 37
Deveaux, (?) (Mrs.) 46
  Cath. 24
Dewar, Ann 43
  Mary 28
Dewick, Hannah 35
Dickert, Eve Margaret 14
  Michael (Sr.) 14
  Peter 14
Dickey, James 26
Dinsley, Ann 21
Dixon, Elizabeth 34
  Mary 21
Dodd, Mary Ann 18
Donavan, Henrietta 17
  Sarah 33
Donnom, Susannah 5
Doughty, Mary 44
Douglas, Mary (Mrs.) 7
Douxaint, Cather. 32
Douxsaint, Jane 41
Doyley, Ann 44
  Elis. 18
  Margt. 44
Drayton, Eliza Elliot 30
Drose, Mary Eli. 12
Dry, Sarah 38
Dryden, Eleanor 5
Drysdel, Mary 13
Dubois, Joanna 15
Dunmire, Elis. 18
Dunn, (?) (Mrs.) 28
Dupont, Ann 12
  Jane 43
Dutarq, Martha 45
Dutarque, Cath. 12
  Mary 22
Eaton, Ann 33
Eberson, Susan 3
Eccles, Elis. (Mrs.) 40
Eddings, Tobitha 45
Edwards, Eliza Hann 15
  James 15
Egan, Jane 21
Elfe, Hannah 3
Elliot, Cath. 31
Elliott, Cath. (Mrs.) 19
  Elis. Burnham 24
  Margt. 10
  Mary 13, 28
  Sabina 20
Ellis, Sabina 33
  Sarah 1
  William 10
Elmour, Catharine (Mrs.) 7
Esmand, Margt. (Mrs.) 21
Estes, Mary (Mrs.) 20
Evans, Esther 42
  Jas. 10
Eveleigh, Thos 43
Fairchild, Ann 43
Farr, Elizabeth 9
Faucheraud, Elis. 18
  Mary 1
Fendin, Dorcas 46

Fenwick, Eliz. 2
  Mary (Mrs.) 11
Fenwicke, Martha 15
  Mary 21
  Sarah 6
Ferguson, Ann 30
  Ester 3
  Jane 44
Ficklin, Mary 22
Field, Sarah (Mrs.) 21
Fitzsimons, Louisa 1
Fleming, Sarah 23
Fletcher, Sarah 29
Fley, Mary 28
Flin, Mary (Mrs.) 42
Foissin, Elizabeth 42
  Susan 19
Forbes, Grace 23
Forcey, Frances 11
Ford, George 43
  Mary 43
  Susanna (Mrs.) 44
Forest, Martha 28
  Mary 2
Foster, Jean 27
  Rebecca Weyman 15
Fowler, Mary 4
Frederick, Elis. 30
  Mary 24
Freer, Elisab. 20
  Jane 23
Frierson, Susanna 28
Fripp, Rebecca 12
  Sarah 13
Frost, Thos. (Rev.) 6
Fuller, Ann 15
  Elis. 26
  Martha 2
  Sarah 30
  Sarah (Mrs.) 20
Fullerton, Sarah (Mrs.) 7
Fyffe, Sarah (Mrs.) 33
Gadsden, Ann 12
  Ann (Mrs.) 25
  Elis 35
Gaillard, Ann 35
  Lidia 12
  Louisa 21
Gallman, Elis. (Mrs.) 20
Garden, Frances 41
Geigleman, Ann 43
George, Sophia 41
Gibbes, Ann 41
  Elisabeth 36
  Mary 19, 28
Gibbons, Mary 18
Gibbs, Alice 20
Gibson, Elis. 31
  Jane 8
Girardeau, Elizabeth 32
Givens, Jane 24
  Martha 13
Glass, Ann 23
Glaze, Ann 13
  Sarah 5

Glen, Charlotte 25
Glover, Mary (Mrs.) 23
Goddin, Amelia 15
Godfrey, Elis. 13
  Mary 3, 37
Golightly, Dorothy 12
  Mary 20
Gord, George 43
  Mary 43
Gordon, Ann 30
  Beatrix 1
  Catherine 32
  Elis. 38
  Frances 42
Gosselin, Magdalen Aimee 1
Gough, Mary 40
Gowdey, Mary Deborah Lee 11
Grace, Catharine (Mrs.) 14
  George 14
Graden, Martha 11
Grange, Mary 11
Graves, Elis. 5
Gray, Agness 44
  Eliza (Mrs.) 40
  Frances 46
  Mary 21
Greaves, Ann 31
Green, Susannah (Mrs.) 20
Greenland, Mary 37
Grimball, Ann (Mrs.) 18
Grimke, Ann 9
  Eliza 35
Guerin, Angelique 8
Guerry, Margt. 40
Guignard, Ann 33
  Frances 21
Gwinnet, Elis. 3
Hall, Caroline 11
  George Abott 11
  Grace 22
Halliday, Deborah 22
  Eliza 25
Haly, Mary (Mrs.) 41
Hamilton, Catharine 33
  Marg. 22
  Mary 40
Hamlin, Mary (Mrs.) 43
Hamon, (?) 27
Hamond, Elis. 2
Hampton, Ann 40
  Martha 23
Harden, Frances 28
  Rebecca 45
Hardy, Mary 3
  Rebecca 45
Harleston, Margaret 9
Hart, Eleanor 36
  Henrietta 27
  Ricksy 36
Hartley, Char. 13
  Mary (Mrs.) 39
Hartman, Susannah 15
Harvey, Elizabeth 31
Hauser, Margaret Christian 1
Hawie, Susannah (Mrs.) 8

Hayne, Mary 31
  Susannah 36
Hazell, Margt. 45
Heath, Thomas 38
Heatly, Rachel 33
Hemingway, William 25
  Wm. 17, 34, 41
Hendlin, Sarah 43
Hennington, Elisabeth 40
Hervey, Ann 27
  Mary 46
Hetherington, Mary (Mrs.) 6
Hext, Ann 41
  Ann (Mrs.) 25
  Jane (Mrs.) 45
Heyward, Margt. 19
Hickey, Mary 13
Hill, Agnus 1
  Ann 11
Himely, Nancy 33
Hinckley, Ann 26
Hinds, Mary 26
  Rebecca 24
  Sarah 32
Hipp, Ann 16
Hippe, Sarah 4
Hixt, Mary (Mrs.) 9
Hodgson, Charlotte 9
Holmes, Elis. 27
  Margaret (Mrs.) 36
  Patience 36
  Rebecca (Mrs.) 12
Holson, Elis. (Mrs.) 18
Holt, William (Rev.) 25, 34
Holwell, Amelia 44
Hoof, Mary 40
Hopton, Alice 32
Horry, Ann 11
  Jonah 11
Hosford, Eliz. 2
Houston, Ann 26
Hoyland, Eleanor 24
Hull, Sarah 38
Hume, Sarah (Mrs.) 32
  Susannah 21
Humphries, Thos. (Rev.) 17
Hunscombe, Ann 34
Hunt, Martha (Mrs.) 35
Hunter, Frances 31
  Helen 31
  Mary (Mrs.) 30
Hutchenson, Rebecca 7
Hutchinson, Ann 7
  Anne Holland 37
Hutson, Eliza. 19
  Esther 45
Hyatt, Mary 4
  Mary (Mrs.) 18
Hyrne, Elis. 42
I'on, Susannah 34
Imer, Jane 14
Immer, Ann (Mrs.) 26
Inglis, Cath. 7
  Elliz 39
Ioor, Mary 43

Ives, Elisabeth 33
Izard, Sarah 6
Izzard, Eliz. 46
Jack, Charity 12
Jackson, Ann 12
  Jane 32
  Mary 4
James, Eleanor 32
  William 43
Jenkins, (?) (Rev.) 37
  Barbara Calder 34
  Micah 34
  Providence (Mrs.) 12
Jennings, Mary 34
Jerdan, Sarah 1
Johnson, Ann (Mrs.) 8, 14
  Dorothy 37
Jones, Amelia 8
  Amelia Rachel 9
  Ann 6
  Dorothy 18
  John 10
  Sarah 16, 25
  Susanh. 29
Joy, Susanna (Mrs.) 9
Kaen, Frances (Mrs.) 44
Keir, Grizel 25
Kerne, Ann Magd. 23
Kilvart, Johanna 41
King, Ann 16
Kinlock, Mary 20
Kirk, Catherine 11
  Charlotte (Mrs.) 19
  Emily Louisa 9
Kirkwood, Elis. (Mrs.) 25
  Jesse (Mrs.) 19
Knowlin, Susannah 12
Knox, Robert 40
La Tour, Angelica 42
Labar, Anne (Mrs.) 33
Ladson, Eliza Ann 44
  James (Maj.) 16
  Mary 7
  Mary (Mrs.) 45
  Sarah Reeve 16
Laird, Sarah 26
Lamboll, Mary 41
Langlois, Cecile 8
Law, Bulah 34
  Mary (Mrs.) 39
Leacroft, Ann 17
Lebby, Ann Haw- 1
Lee, Harriet 20
Legare, Amy 2
  Elizabeth 36
  James 20
  Mary 11
  Sarah 20, 39
Leger, Eliza. 9
Lennox, Charlotte 29
  Mary 41
Lenoir, Leah (Mrs.) 26
Lesesne, Ann 25, 43
  Elis. 3, 5
  Susannah 19

Lewis, Sarah 37
Lind, Catherine (Mrs.) 4
Linning, Eliz. 34
Liston, Isabella 10
Little, Hester 39
Livingston, Ann 7
  Sarah (Mrs.) 30
Lloyd, Elis. 4
  Eliza 14
  Rebecca 6, 10
  Sarah 6
Lockhart, Margaret 5
Loretz, Andrew (Rev.) 14
Love, Elizabeth Cath. 17
  Mary Rose 23
Lowndes, Amarinthia 35
  Sarah (Mrs.) 31
Lynch, Elis. 18
  Hannah 29
  Sabina 7
M'Gilvray, Eliz (Mrs.) 34
M'Grath, Hannah 36
M'Pherson, (?) (Mrs.) 28
Mackey, Mary (Mrs.) 36
Maguire, Mary 13
Maine, Esther 21
Mann, Ann 6
  Eleanor (Mrs.) 24
Marion, Ann 34
  Mary 22
Maronett, Ann 45
Martin, Elis. (Mrs.) 5
  John 10
  Magdalen 29
  Sebina 28
Mathewes, Ann 17
  Ann (Mrs.) 15
  Charl. (Mrs.) 37
  Lois 18
  Martha 27
  Susannah 18
Mathews, Elisa. 19
Matthews, Peggy 36
Maybank, Hannah (Mrs.) 16
Mazyck, Charlotte 7
  Mary Ann 44
  Sylvia 29
McAllister, Cath Othelia
  (Mrs.) 4
McAlpin, Gilbert 25
McBride, Archd 25
  Jane 8
McCall, Mary 7
McCartey, (?) (Mrs.) 30
McCinny, Caty 2
McClintock, Jane 1
McCullock, Polly 3
McDonald, Sarah 23
McGaw, Ann 30
  Sarah 45
McKensie, Ann 37
  Sarah (Mrs.) 3
McKenzie, Mary 22
McKewn, Mary 35
  Sarah 18, 22

Pounds, Mary 41
Powell, Sarah 40
Poyas, Eliza Catharine 2
Price, Elizabeth (Mrs.) 14
Prince, Sarah 40
Prioleau, Jane Rebecca 5
  Margt. 14
  Mary 17
  Sarah (Mrs.) 35
Pritchard, Ann 33
Purry, Eleanor 5
Quash, Elizabeth 31
Quince, (?) 33
Radcliffe, Eliz. 36
Rake, Mary (Mrs.) 45
Randall, Dorcas 23
Rantowle, Eleanor 33
Raven, Elizabeth 42
  Henrietta (Mrs.) 39
Reeve, Elizabeth Abel 44
Reeves, Sarah 15
Reid, Elis. 5
  Susan. (Mrs.) 22
Reily, Eliza 6
Remington, Ann 6
Richards, Sarah 43
Richardson, Susan 38
Richbourg, James (Jr.) 16
  John 16
  William 16
Righton, Jane 28
Rippon, Mary 18
Rivers, Elis. 36
  Elizabeth 16
  Love 40
  Mary 24, 45
  Rachel 39
  Rebecca 34
  Rizpah 46
Roberts, Ann (Mrs.) 42
Roche, Eliza. 29
  Mary 28
Rodgaman, Ann 1
Rogers, Mary (Mrs.) 16
Rolles, Cather. 8
Roper, Ann 45
  Martha 39
Rose, Esther 41
  Hepsibah 7
Rosse, Eliz. (Mrs.) 3
Rowel, Ann 30
Runnel, Mary 24
Russell, Alicia 27
  Elis. (Mrs.) 21
Rutledge, Elis. (Mrs.) 14
  Jane 27
  Mary 38
Sabb, Ann 19
  Deborah 40
Saltus, Mary 27
Sams, Sarah 27
Samways, Martha 35
Sandaford, Elis. 3
Sanders, Ann (Mrs.) 2
  Elis. 17

Sanders (cont.)
  Ezekiel 26
  Mary Ann Clerk 34
Sands, Hannah (Mrs.) 19
Sanks, Mary 5
Sarrazin, Eliza. 33
Sarsedas, Rebecca 8
Saunders, Elis. 7
  Eliza. 35
Schwartzkop, Mary (Mrs.) 32
Scott, Elis. (Mrs.) 3
  Jane 30
  Sally 27
  Susannah 39
Screven, Martha 2
Sergeant, Eliza 24
Shackleford, Sarah (Mrs.) 45
  Susannah 40
Shands, Lucy 25
Shanks, Martha 26
Sharp, Mary 22
Shehevral, Mary 37
Shoemaker, Rebecca 43
Shubrick, Elizabeth 25
  Hannah 19
  Mary 13
  Sarah 38
Simkins, Ann 2
Simmons, (?) (Mrs.) 41
  Ann 13
  Elizabeth 19
  Rachel 5
Simons, J. Dewar (Rev.) 20
  Martha 17
  Mary 37
  Mary Read 37
  Rebecca 21
  Sarah 5
  Thos. 37
Sinclair, Ann 19
  Mary 15
Singellton, Rebecca 8
Singletary, Hester 30
Singleton, Richd. 16
  Sarah 16
Slappy, George 38
Slater, Frances Ann 7
Sleigh, Ann 36
  Elizabeth 24
Smelie, Sarah (Mrs.) 33
Smiser, Dorothy 1
Smith, Ann 10, 22, 43
  Anna Maris 26
  Cat. 16
  Catherine 24
  Elis. 26
  Elis. (Mrs.) 13
  Elisabeth (Mrs.) 8
  Elizabeth 28
  Hezekiah 13, 16, 30
  Judith 23
  Livingston 31
  Margt. 34
  Martha 4
  Mary 9, 20, 40

Williams (cont.)
  Ann 45
  Margt. 32
  Mary 26
Williamson, Charlotte (Mrs.)
    43
  Lizey 9
Willis, Jane 45
  Mary (Mrs.) 41
Willson, John 41
  Martha 41
  Saml. 16
Wilson, Mary M. 43
  Sarah 14, 23
Winborn, Elis. 42
Winburn, Mary 44
Winwood, (?) (Mrs.) 19
Wood, Elis. (Mrs.) 29
  Elizabeth 6
Woodcroft, Martha 27
Woodward, Charlotte 26
  William 26
Wragg, Ann 14, 15
  Henrietta 46
  Mary 27
Wrainch, Ann Eliza 30
Yorston, Jean 41
Young, Elis. 28
  Jane 38
  Margaret 40

www.ingramcontent.com/pod-product-compliance
Lightning Source LLC
Chambersburg PA
CBHW052107270326
41931CB00012B/2920